HAUNTED VERMONT

Thomas D'Agostino & Arlene Nicholson

Photography by Arlene Nicholson

4880 Lower Valley Road, Atglen, PA 19310 USA

Schiffer Books are available at special discounts for bulk purchases for sales promotions or premiums. Special editions, including personalized covers, corporate imprints, and excerpts can be created in large quantities for special needs. For more information contact the publisher:

Published by Schiffer Publishing Ltd.
4880 Lower Valley Road
Atglen, PA 19310
Phone: (610) 593-1777;
Fax: (610) 593-2002
E-mail: Info@schifferbooks.com

For the largest selection of fine reference books on this and related subjects, please visit our website at **www.schifferbooks.com**

We are always looking for people to write books on new and related subjects. If you have an idea for a book please contact us at the above address.

This book may be purchased
from the publisher.
Include $5.00 for shipping.
Please try your bookstore first.

You may write for a free catalog.

In Europe, Schiffer books
are distributed by
Bushwood Books
6 Marksbury Ave.
Kew Gardens
Surrey TW9 4JF England
Phone: 44 (0) 20 8392-8585;
Fax: 44 (0) 20 8392-9876
E-mail: info@bushwoodbooks.co.uk
Website: www.bushwoodbooks.co.uk

Dedication

I dedicate this book to my sister and guardian angel, Diane Mary D'Agostino who is at all times watching over us. You are always in our hearts and will never be forgotten.

Acknowledgements

Special thanks goes out to Joe Citro whose knowledge of the other side of Vermont is far beyond legend itself. Mandy Pincins and Justin Badorek. Special thanks also goes out to Robert Hughes and Victoria Julian. While roving the Vermont countryside in search of the perfect wedding destination, the couple also carried their ghost hunting equipment with them, stayed at, and investigated many of the places in this book. They even recorded some EVPs while in a few of the haunted locations. Lori and John DaSilva, who also ventured across the Vermont terrain. Their photos and stories are also a great asset to this book. Ron Kolek and Ron Kolek Jr. of New England Ghost Project, Dinah Roseberry, Matthew Moniz, Christopher Balzano, C.P.E.A.R. paranormal group, Jeff Belanger, Paul and Ben Eno, everyone at the White House in Wilmington, Michael Reynolds of the River Mist Bed and Breakfast, Bailey's Mill, John Barwick and John Barwick Jr., everyone at the Equinox Resort, The Green Mountain Inn, The Dorset Inn and all those who wished to remain anonymous but were instrumental in the making of this book.

Contents

Prologue

Let me state for the record that Arlene and I are, first and foremost, paranormal investigators. There has, however always been the need to share our knowledge of historical and haunted places with those who wished to travel the countryside looking for ghosts, legends, and folklore. That is mainly how our books came to be. *Haunted Vermont,* along with the previous tomes we have written, are designed to guide the adventurer through the world of paranormal wonders that abound New England. The goal was not so much writing a fictional novel in hopes of giving people nightmares as it was putting forth a large volume of haunted places that include some history and their haunts to be preserved and relished for the future. Each book contains stories from their respective states and regions where the reader may spend more time visiting the places and experiencing the wonder that awaits them rather then just reading about it in dull minute detail. We always try to keep a little left over for the reader to experience and discover for themselves some of the history and mystery each place holds. That is the beauty of legend tripping and adventure.

It became evident to me long ago that people wanted an opportunity to visit haunted places and perhaps see something move by unseen hands or hear a voice from beyond, or maybe even see a ghost or two. In all our books, Arlene and I have done just that. They are your personal encyclopedia; state by state, region by region, to haunted New England complete with history, haunts, and directions. There are no embellishments as the facts of the haunts speak for themselves. This is especially true if you are fortunate enough to witness a paranormal occurrence in one of the many sites we have penned onto paper.

I have experimented with different writing styles in order to try more diverse fashions of prose. Some may have approved of this idea while others prefer a more modern status quo form of narration. This does not take away from the fact that the haunts and legends are there awaiting your arrival in either body or just spirit.

This continuing series takes the reader, legend tripper, and paranormal adventurer into Vermont. The Green Mountain State is rich with wild tales and unique haunts that make for great reading and even greater firsthand excursions to the places within this book. Because all of our books have been geared towards the reader going out and visiting the places themselves, we have finally decided to include a special section on how to perform a more successful paranormal investigation. This is a valuable primer that covers some history, types of haunts, equipment, and tips on how to capture EVPs and photos of paranormal activity. It will be a beneficial guide to anyone seeking paranormal activity while at the places Arlene and I have visited, investigated, and written about.

Introduction

I must admit that although I had contemplated a book on haunted Vermont, I was not so sure it would be a lucrative venture. My friend, Skip Gervais, handed me some haunted places in Vermont he acquired from the internet. "Just in case you decide to write a book on Vermont," he said. It was as if he was waiting for me to add another tome to his collection.

As I read them I became intrigued by some of the narratives I perused. They were not your everyday ordinary New England haunts, not by a long stretch. There was much more to these legends than just ghosts roaming the halls of a home or college dormitory.

With those few pages and the kind assistance from esteemed Vermont author Joseph Citro, I made up my mind to write *Haunted Vermont*. The fact that one side of my family originally hails from the Green Mountain State (Swanton to be exact) was another factor that made me want to delve into the haunted heritage that Vermont has to offer.

Vermonters are very matter-of-fact about their ghosts. When most people shudder or run for the hills at the notion of a haunt, "Green Mountaineers" simply say, "Oh that's just our ghost." They seem to treat their ghosts, guests, and grandmothers with the same love and compassion that make them so interesting to converse with or listen to their narratives. Some of those stories rival and even surpass the best ghost stories ever penned onto a piece of parchment. A quantity of these tales may seem beyond belief, but then again, that's what makes them supernatural.

From Frozen citizens, haunted bridges, creepy colleges, to vampires, strange creatures, and every character in between, Vermont has a stunning array of haunts and history that makes for one very special road trip. Whether you enjoy just perusing these pages for entertainment or feel the need to seek out the Vermont "spirit," this book will be a handy guide to ghostly fun.

BELLOWS FALLS

The River Mist Bed and Breakfast

Bellows Falls is a bucolic little hamlet with a heap of history predating the arrival of the Europeans. Native Indians saw the falls as a plentiful source of food. They would migrate there to camp and catch the abundant salmon and shad that made their way up the river in their undying quest to ascend the falls. Soon other settlers found refuge in Bellows Falls and began building their homes there. It was these brave pioneers who also built the first bridge to cross the Connecticut River in 1785. One of the first canals in the United States was erected there in 1802 as an attempt to bypass the falls. As a result of this, Bellows Falls became one of the most important railroad stops in Northern New England. In the 1870s, paper mills began to use wood pulp instead of rags as raw material in the making of paper. The paper mills of Bellows Falls were among the first of these industries to make that important transition.

The town still retains its historic integrity with the preservation of many buildings, thus making it an important historical place to tour and learn about the early days of the industrial revolution in addition to the subsequent settlements that sprang up along the rivers of our great nation.

While visiting, there is one place that holds some of Bellows Falls past within its walls, a past that just might pay you a visit in the dark hours. It is called The River Mist Bed and Breakfast.

The River Mist exudes the charm and loveliness of a Victorian-era Vermont-style bed and breakfast. Innkeeper Michael Reynolds spares no expense in making sure his guests are treated with the utmost reverence. That goes for the eternal ones as well. The inn has had a few old souls lingering for quite some time. They are friendly but do like to play tricks now and then. I talked with Michael and he sent me this story. I will leave it as he told it so you, the reader, can get the most accurate first hand accounts of the ghosts at the River Mist.

We've always preferred to believe that the cause of the strange occurrences in our home was Mrs. Clark, the nice little old lady who died peacefully dozing off in the parlor while having lunch with her minister, but the mischievousness nature of the haunting and menacing feeling often associated with it makes me wonder if perhaps a less benign spirit is at work here.

Shortly after moving in, my gold nugget and diamond ring came up missing. It had last been on the bedside table of the Garden Room where I had removed it before going to sleep. The next day it was gone. An expensive piece of jewelry, we searched and searched for over six months with no luck. When at last we'd nearly forgotten about it, my partner Roger went up to the attic one day to retrieve an item that had yet to be unpacked since our move from California. He removed the tape from the box and was shocked to find my ring sealed inside, lying right atop the other items in the box. We've never been able to imagine how the ring got inside a sealed box, but somehow it had traveled by unseen hands up one flight of stairs and defied natural laws, passing through sturdy cardboard and packing tape, resting squarely centered upon a bundle of miscellaneous things that hadn't seen the light of day since being packed up six

months prior in a house over 3,000 miles away.

This seemed to be the dramatic beginning of a string of disturbances. We felt a presence. To those who have never experienced this, it is like the feeling a person gets when they are being watched; as though someone has crept up silently behind them and somehow you feel their nearness ... you turn to look, and your suspicions are affirmed—there is indeed someone there. Being in the presence of a spirit is no different from being in the presence of a person—the only thing that is missing is a physical body. Like people, some spirits are kind, caring, crabby, mean-spirited, affable, silly, or downright evil. You can also tend to experience a range of different feelings and subsequent behaviors, as people are multidimensional beings, they do not cease to be this way after they have passed from the physical state.

Shadows passing across walls, footsteps down halls, chilly spots in otherwise warm rooms, and faraway voices just slightly out of the range of distinguishable were experienced by not only we Innkeepers, but our guests as well. Several times when Roger was making the bed in the Garden Room, a mischievous spirit "flicked" him in the back of the head. I am of the mind that if a house is occupied by the souls of people who once lived there, as prior owners they, in a sense, have more right to be here than I. Knowing this, Roger spoke aloud to the spirit, and laid down some ground rules: They were welcome to stay so long as they didn't frighten our guests.

From that day things became very quiet for a while. But eventually, a guest commented on seeing a dark shadow cross the walls of her room. Having violated our agreement, Roger told the spirit (or spirits) they would have to leave. We have had no incidents since that time, other than the typical noises associated with an old house.

The River Mist was originally the Thompson House; built in 1895 by a railroad engineer for the Boston and Main. The couple had no children, nor did any other owners after them up until 1986. Because the house has so many rooms that were not being used, it was utilized as a guesthouse since its beginning.

There is one other possible prior resident with a less pleasant history than that of Mrs. Clark who might also be responsible for the disturbances. He was a man by the name of John who moved from the house shortly after his wife died. He rented a hotel room downtown, just across the street from the hardware store where he worked. He had recently been diagnosed with a fatal illness, and steeped in depression and grief, shot himself to death. His coworkers discovered the grisly scene in the back room of the hardware store when they arrived for work in the morning...

So, there you have it right from the person who would know best, other than the actual spirits that is. The only way to get a better account of the inn is to stay a night. Even if you don't encounter a ghost, there are a lot of other adventures to partake, such as hiking, sightseeing, and shopping. Michael also serves one of the best breakfast spreads in the state so everyone is guaranteed a wonderful stay at the River Mist. (No wonder some have never left.)

THE RIVER MIST BED & BREAKFAST

7 Burt Street
Bellows Falls, VT 05101
(802) 463-9023

Take I-91 to Exit 5, Bellows Falls. Bear right onto access road. Take left at stop sign onto Route 5 and proceed about 4 miles into the village of Bellows. Falls. Take Burt Street and the River Mist is third house from the corner on the right.

Rockingham Meeting House

While we were on the subject of haunted places, Michael Reynolds also included this little tidbit in his relation of the River Mist. Again, I will let his words be your guide.

Another place that has a lot of activity is the Rockingham Meeting House, just a few miles east of the Village of Bellows Falls. It is the best-preserved example of a eighteenth-century meeting house in all of New England. It is still in completely original condition, never having had heat or electricity added to the building. The old lady who works there seasonally to keep the building open for tourists and visitors allows me to play the pump organ. One day when my brother was visiting from California, I took him to see the meetinghouse. As I was playing the organ, using only the keys in the center of the keyboard, I was amused to notice that the upper keys were playing along with me by unseen hands!

We then went upstairs to the loft, where far down the aisle of cubicles one of the stall doors suddenly swung open by itself. I whispered to my brother to take notice, as I didn't want to frighten the little old lady who spends long hours alone in the building. The place, being built for acoustics, carried my voice, and she called up to us from the first floor, "Oh, nothing you say will surprise me. One day my little grandson and granddaughter spent the day with me, and the full apparition of a woman appeared to my granddaughter outside in the graveyard: It scared her so badly she refuses ever to come up here again."

I've also noticed that a lot of orbs show up in photos at the meetinghouse. The Meetinghouse was built in 1787 and remains mostly unaltered from its original construction. It is presently the oldest building in Vermont that is still in use as a public meeting place.

Imagine a place where the spirits of yore get to live in the same conditions as when they were gracing this earth in the physical body. It must be a treat to haunt so simply without all the modern amenities to have to manipulate for attention. Perhaps it could be a bit more challenging for them to have to be more imaginative as there are no lights to turn on or off. But then there is the pump organ to animate with ethereal music or the ghosts can extinguish a candle or two. Better yet, relighting one is certainly apt to make a believer out of many who pour forth through the threshold of the ancient edifice.

If you find yourself a few miles east of the Village of Bellows Falls and you hear the sound of an organ coming from an old meetinghouse, or the misty figure of a woman meandering among the headstones, don't be alarmed for they are just feeling at home in a place where time and progress has left alone.

THE ROCKINGHAM MEETINGHOUSE

Meetinghouse Road
Bellows Falls, Vermont 05101

Take Exit 6 off of I-91 for US-5/ Rockingham. Bear left onto US-5 and continue onto VT-103N for 1.4 miles. Take a left onto Meetinghouse Road.

Bennington Monument

BENNINGTON

Bennington College

Some ghosts seem to enjoy being seen as well as heard. Others never make as much as a peep in front of the living. Then there are those elusive noises that echo down the halls of buildings but are never accompanied by any visible countenance. These pesky demons of din are the most mysterious of all due to the fact that they never leave a visual apparition to identify them by. They creep around unseen creating thumps, bangs, and otherworldly articulations that make the very flesh of the living quiver and their hairs stand on end. A stunned recipient might turn towards the noise with a start and realize there is no physical origin that could initiate the baleful clamor from the other side.

Such is the case with Jennings Hall at Bennington College.

The Unknown Spirits of Jennings Hall

The beautiful three-story granite mansion was once the home of Frederick Beach Jennings and his wife, Laura. According to historical records, Frederick married Laura Hall Park on July 27, 1880. Their wedding was a grand affair, an event to match any Bennington had seen in recent times with many notable citizens in attendance. Music and gaiety filled the atmosphere of this posh nuptial where the guests left their hectic lives for a short spell to relish in the couple's union. Frederick was the son of Reverend Dr. Isaac Jennings of Bennington and Laura was the granddaughter of ex-governor Hiland Hall. Frederick was a very successful attorney. This is evident by the lavish mansion he once owned that graces the charming environ of the college to this day. He died on Wednesday, May 26, 1920, after suffering a brain stroke the previous Sunday, and was buried in Old Bennington Cemetery.

In 1931, Mrs. Jennings donated a section of the surrounding farmland for the use of a college that was in the process of being founded. The school was an establishment of higher education for girls. In 1932, the first class of eighty-seven young women began their inaugural semester at the newly formed Bennington College for Arts, Science, and Humanities. Bennington College is reported to be the first college to include liberal and performing arts in its curriculum. At the time, the main educational building was a barn that had been meticulously renovated by craftsmen who had become unemployed due to the stock market crash of 1929. This barn is still in use today and still carries the moniker it was christened with way back when. It shows up on the campus map as simply, "The Barn."

The barn still tenants many of the classrooms along with administrative offices. Most of the classrooms are on the second floor of this beautiful expansive structure that once housed dairy cows. The smooth wooden floors and Tudor windows are a prime example of the wealth that the Jennings possessed.

In 1935, males were allowed into the theater program as it became obvious that men were needed for certain performances. It was not until 1969 that the college went completely co-ed. It now ranks as one of the countries top private institutions for higher learning. Such notable figures as dancer/choreographer Martha Graham, novelists Bernard Malamud and John Gardner, composer Allen Shawn, sculptor Anthony Caro, jazz musician Milford Graves, and Pulitzer Prize poets Stanley Kunitz, Mary Oliver, Theodore Roethke, and Anne Waldman have not only graced the halls of Bennington College as students, but have gone on to become educators there as well. There are also some spirits that have gained global fame that wish to remain anonymous, at least in description. These entities reside in the Jennings manor that now houses the music department. The ornate staircases and beautifully appointed rooms are alive with students and sounds of music during the day but after the sun's rays have quit the horizon, it is time for the resonance of those from the other side of the veil to bring forth their concerts of echoes and voices.

Students who dare venture forth unaccompanied through the threshold of the old manor will find themselves in the thick of the unknown. Mysterious footsteps permeate the halls, yet there is not a soul around to initiate them, at least not a living soul. Their reverberations are obviously from a time and entity long past. Then there are the voices; phantom conversations that transcend the barriers of death to once more be heard among the living. Students have actually entered rooms where instruments are poised on their stands only to become unnerved and make a hasty exit as the apparatus comes to life with the ethereal sounds perpetuated by some invisible force. The night is the spirits' time to commence their phantom opuses and they do it well. So well, that the mansion is documented as being an inspirational force for the novel, *The Haunting of Hill House* by Shirley Jackson.

BENNINGTON COLLEGE

One College Drive
Bennington, VT 05201

Take I-90 West to Lee/Lenox, MA (Exit 2). Follow signs to Route 7/20 North to Pittsfield. Take U.S. Route 7 North to Bennington. At the intersection of Route 7 and Route 9 stay straight on Route 7 North. Continue on Route 7 North through two sets of lights; after the second set of lights, continue straight through on Route 7 North. Take the first left to Route 67A and exit right to Route 67A (Bennington/North Bennington). At end of exit ramp (at light), take a left onto Route 67A North. Follow for less than a mile (Home Depot is on your right). After second set of lights, the College entrance is on the right.

Southern Vermont College

If anything, Bennington seems to have a lot of spirited places of higher education. It is likely due to the fact that some of the buildings on the campuses were once private mansions that still thrive with the revenants of past owners. If this is so, then Southern Vermont College's main architectural attraction, the Everett Mansion has some very interesting and historical ghosts roaming its vast halls; namely Edward Everett himself.

Edward Everett was born on May 18, 1851. He began his career as a bottle salesman for his stepfather but soon became shareholder, then owner of the American Bottle Company. His knack for making money brought him to Ohio

Everett Mansion at Southern Vermont College where the ghosts of Edward Everett and his first and second wives still roam the halls.

where he found large deposits of gas and oil. This discovery and innovative improvements in the manufacturing of glass made him a very wealthy man. His company would later merge with another perennial mogul called Corning. This became the Owens-Corning Fiberglass Company.

In 1910, Everett purchased 500 acres along the slopes of Mount Anthony and began construction on his summer villa. From 1911 to 1914, work crews meticulously toiled under the architectural direction of George Totten, the Gilded Age's most skilled architect. Thirty stonemasons from Italy worked seven days a week for six months straight to complete the goldstone exterior of the mansion. The red roof tiles and marble for the stairs and fireplaces were imported from Italy, the mahogany paneling came from Cuba, and the crystal and silver appointments were shipped over from England. The twenty-seven-room mansion was furnished in lavish Victorian décor with parquet floors of various beautiful designs in different wood. The grand oak staircase still adorns the entrance of the building as one walks through the doors from the patio. No expense was spared in creating this beautiful manor where the Everett family could spend their summers overlooking the mountains from the high elevation the patriarch of the family had chosen for the site of the mansion. The house cost two million dollars to construct. Not a lot of money when you figure Mr.

Everett's wealth was about forty to fifty million dollars.

It was then called the "Orchard House" as it was surrounded by one of the largest apple orchards in the country. About 75,000 apple trees graced the countryside along with 3,000 plum trees and 2,000 quince trees that Mr. Everett dutifully planted. Edward, his wife, Amy, and their three daughters moved into the house in 1915. In 1917, his wife, Amy, tragically died after a prolonged illness.

He soon met up with another woman named Grace Burnap who was thirty years his younger. They married in 1920 and had two daughters together. Edward died in April of 1929 at the age of 77. His death led to a quarrel over the estate called "The Battle of Bennington Millions" where his first three daughters sued Grace for a larger share of their father's inheritance. The daughters claimed he was not of sound mind when he wrote out the will giving them but one-tenth of his wealth and the rest bequeathed to Grace and her daughters. The 1930 battle was one of the most famous in Vermont history. The court finally agreed to overturn the will and award the daughters each one-fifth of the inheritance while Grace and her daughters received the other two-thirds.

Grace lived in the mansion until 1952 before selling it to the Order of the Holy Cross. The order then exchanged properties with Southern Vermont College; then named St. Josephs College

One of the grand hallways of Everett Mansion where the ghosts are seen.

in downtown Bennington in 1974. The Sisters of St. Joseph had established the college as St. Joseph's Business School in 1926.

The mansion now houses the administrative offices, library, bookstore, café, art gallery, mailroom, dark room, and a classroom. It also houses a few ghosts that do not mind making their presence known. Arlene and I visited the college on a beautiful May afternoon. The manor had looked much like it did in its heyday; the ornate woodwork, grand oak staircase, patios and stunning views of the surrounding area were all breathtaking. The semester had ended and the empty halls and rooms afforded us an opportunity to take some pictures and record EVPs. Although we did not capture any activity on film or recorder, we did get an opportunity to chat with a few people who were still on campus and they were gracious in sharing the stories of the college and its array of haunts. Here is what we heard and what we have read as well.

Everett's second wife, Grace is seen gliding through the halls and rooms of the estate. Some claim that the spirit of Everett's first wife also resides within the stone edifice. She is known as the "Lady in White" as she is spied in a white robe while floating through the manor. Edward's ghost has also been reported in the house. Much of the strange occurrences at the Everett estate are comprised of wisps of smoke on the stage, doorknobs turning, lights turning on and off by themselves, and doors that were previously locked mysteriously flying wide open. Then there are the shadows that cross the halls and the footsteps that echo in the otherwise empty building.

The shade of a monk in a black robe has been witnessed floating around the perimeter of the campus. The property was a seminary once so the presence of such a spirit would not be so out of the ordinary. Many legends abound of the hooded figure as he roams the grounds only to vanish before anyone can get close to him. As to the identity of the strange shade, that is still a mystery to be solved.

The old carriage house is now a computer lab. This is where a man in period clothing is seen wandering around. Doors also lock by themselves and computers turn off suddenly. The carriage house used to accommodate the Everett's Rolls Royce automobiles while also serving as living quarters for the coachmen. With the diverse array of paranormal activity it must be a very exciting school both for the living and otherwise.

SOUTHERN VERMONT COLLEGE

982 Mansion Drive
Bennington, Vermont 05201

Take Route 7 to Elm Street in Bennington. Turn left onto Monument Avenue then take 2nd right onto Regwood Avenue. Take immediate left onto Mansion Drive and follow to parking lot.

Looking out upon the mountains from the grounds of the Everett Estate.

BRATTLEBORO

St. Michael's Church

This next story is quite an out of the ordinary little tale, even for the best "yarners" Vermont has to offer. It has been told throughout the ages and ne'er a word has been changed, as there is not much to add. It stands by itself as one of those narratives that is a true Vermont legend.

St. Michael's Church in downtown Brattleboro had an organist who was not only a talented musician but very affable with the parishioners as well. The congregation always looked forward to hearing his music during the Sunday service and engaging in many an interesting and enchanting conversation with him afterward. They liked him so much, that when he died, they built a mausoleum for him where they then propped him up with his favorite organ.

It was not long after that they began to hear strange sounds emanating from the churchyard. Low musical utterances that sounded much like the baffled notes of a church organ. The sounds continued until someone discovered that it was coming from the former organist's burial chamber. This would have pleased the parishioners much that their favorite organist was, in death, still doing what he loved in life, but there was one problem. He seemed to have lost his touch for the instrument as now, harsh and discordant notes echoed through the air sending those within an earshot of them to wince and scurry for more silent surroundings.

Finally, a few brave souls dared to open the crypt in an attempt to see what really was happening. They surreptitiously approached the vault and slowly opened the door not knowing what to expect. The notes droned in their ears as they made the final thrust that dislodged the rusty partition from its frame and entered the chamber. What they saw next was quite a shock to them. There sat the organist propped up at the instrument. Scurrying among the keys were rats that had been feeding upon his fingers while also pushing down upon the ivory slats thus creating the awful music that had been pervading through the midnight air.

St. Michael's Church

Walnut Street in Brattleboro (The Cemetery is located off Oak Grove Avenue)

Whether these are the actual locations has never been made clear. Visit the place for yourself and see what you may uncover. That is part of the fun of visiting haunted places, the adventure of discovering things for yourself.

Brattleboro Country Club

While closing the dining area, a muffled utterance suddenly echoes through the air. Looking around, the staff member notices there is no one in the room or in the area above the dining chamber. Yet, the voice, though inarticulate was quite audible. This is a common occurrence rumored to happen at the Brattleboro Country Club. The waitresses do not like to close the dining room alone knowing that at any time, the phantom voice might fill the room and them with trepidation.

The voice is not the only strange sound heard at the club. Footsteps are also heard overhead when the area is otherwise empty. Other various odd sounds have been noted in the building which are not the normal dins of daily routine. No one knows the identity of the ghost or ghosts that still take up residence there but they are harmless and prefer not to be seen, only heard from time to time.

The original club dates back to 1913 when pro golfer Tom McNamara made plans for a nine-hole golf course. The club was incorporated and opened for members in 1914. It is a privately owned and operated establishment.

Historic Holton Hall is reported to be home to a few spirits of the past.

BRATTLEBORO COUNTRY CLUB

Dummerston Road
in Brattleboro

Being a private club, permission
to enter must be obtained before
visiting.

Austine School for the Deaf

While traveling on I-91 in Brattleboro, the Austine School is easy to spot as it sits perched up high and well marked on a hill above the thoroughfare. It is quite a piece of architecture. The building, officially called Holton Hall, is a historic landmark. The school, which was established in 1904 and opened its doors in 1912, came about by the generosity of Colonel William Austine.

Since then, the campus has grown into a welcoming facility for learning—so welcoming that a few spirits may be still enjoying the atmosphere. Security and staff members have heard their names called in a certain area when there is no one around at all to beckon them. Other noises are heard as well. Lights turn on and off by themselves and people get the feeling they are being followed. Shadow people have also been reported darting from one place to another. Perhaps it might be the Colonel periodically checking up on his dowry.

The school is a private school and permission should be sought to visit.

BRISTOL

Bristol Notch

Blood curdling screams echo through the woods followed by the ominous howling of a dog, yet there is no one who would dare venture into the vicinity where these unearthly sounds emanate. First there are the many shafts that have been burrowed over the centuries by prospectors in search of a lost treasure, then, of course, there are the ghosts. The accounts that have been penned in regard to the origin of the Bristol silver mine vary but the end result is that one of the shafts is haunted.

According to an account in Robert Ellis Cahill's book, *New England's Mountain Madness*, three Spaniards came to Bristol just after the Revolutionary War and discovered the large vein of silver in the South Mountains. They left as quietly as they came, but soon returned with two women and a boy named Philip DeGrau. They mined the silver and hid it in a nearby cave after smelting it into bars. (Smelting separates the lead from the silver and it is estimated that prehistoric man was performing this procedure as early as 3000 B.C.)

Other recants of the legend begin to converge here. The Vermont winters are very harsh and arrive much earlier in the year than most places in New England. The snow begins to fall early and keeps falling well into the spring. This was not part of their plan and they knew they could not stay at the mine to brave the fierce winter that beckoned upon their door. The miners had to leave but vowed to wait until all three were ready to return together the next spring in order to bring their riches back to the old country. The cave selected was covered with rock, mud and brush as to completely mask its whereabouts and their hoard of silver from nosy intruders. It seems that many of the villagers were very interested in the stranger's digging about in their woods. One writing pens that they were actually forced out of the township by the residents resulting in them having to hide the silver until a time when they could sneak back and take their fortune with them.

23

BRISTOL

For some reason or other none of them ever returned to claim their cache. It was Philip DeGrau who returned some eighteen years later, but time had been cruel to his memory and the landscape. Using what little landmarks he remembered, he tried to find the cave but after months of searching, he had to abandon his quest for the silver bars and return to Spain for the winter. He too, never returned. He did, however, mention his purpose to a few townsfolk and that was enough to send the town into "silver rush" frenzy.

Before long, treasure seekers had burrowed scores of holes and shafts into the earth and rock around South Mountain. Some Canadian entrepreneurs started a business venture in 1840 in attempt to excavate the silver stash but were also unsuccessful in finding the lost cave or any rich vein of silver running through the mountain. Even now, treasure hunters scour the vicinity of South Mountain and the Bristol cliff in hopes of striking it rich yet no one has ever found the hidden hoard. The shafts, some 100 feet deep, remain as a vestige to those who have searched in vain over the last few centuries in search of the precious grayish-white metallic chemical element known as silver, or *Ag* on the elemental chart. There is one shaft that everyone avoids and with good sense and reason. It is the bore that is so aptly named "The Ghost Shaft of Bristol Notch."

Early in the twentieth century, a boy and his dog were out in the woods around the shafts. While playing among the rocks, the little boy somehow fell into one of the deep caverns and could not climb back out. He was not discovered until weeks later when his dog was found dead at the entrance of the shaft. Forever loyal, the pooch stayed with his master to the end.

Now on those frigid Vermont nights when the wind picks up, screams mixed with the blustery gusts can be heard followed by an ethereal howling that reverberates around the mountain. Locals know all too well that they are hearing the terrifying wails of the ghosts of Bristol Notch.

If you decide to go in search of the lost treasure heed well these words, for the dreadful cries of the two ghosts are enough to make one turn and seek safer ground.

BRISTOL NOTCH

The notch is south of town.

Burlington
Photo courtesy of Victoria Julian.

BURLINGTON

The Ice House

Burlington is located in the northwestern tip of the state along the famed Lake Champlain, home of "Champ" the lakes infamous sea creature. It is also home for many land bound oddities and eerie places.

One such place is called the Ice House, a noted restaurant and office building complex located along the shore of Lake Champlain in the downtown area.

Arlene's daughter, Mandy, and her fiancé, Justin, had removed to Burlington due to her work with a company she had been employed with for many years. Being a chef, Justin sought employment at restaurants in the area and was given a job at the Ice House Restaurant. It wasn't very long before he had many a tale to relate to me.

One day as Justin was in the kitchen cleaning up, he spied someone out of the corner of his eye. A bit startled and more curious, turned around and his eyes transfixed upon a semi-transparent apparition of an old lady swinging a bell. He immediately noticed that the bell made no noise whatsoever. At that point, he knew he was staring at an image from another place in time. As he approached the figure, it vanished as silently as it came. The wraith has been seen numerous times by other employees as well. A cook who has been there for many years is so accustomed to the haunted place that it seems lonely to him without something happening regularly.

The staff on duty has often heard the distinct sound of ice blocks being dragged across the floor. The grinding sound becomes an eerie echo in their ears until the ghostly labor has ended and silence once again prevails. The original structure served as a storage facility for the large blocks of ice cut from the lake. It is told that the great blocks of ice sliding or falling accidentally crushed many laborers of the icehouse. Some of them were badly maimed while others died. It is no wonder the place harbors residual energy in the form of spirits not ready to leave the place where they spent their possible final earthly moments. Objects that are put down in obvious places tend to disappear only to be later discovered hidden in strange nooks of the kitchen and basement. The long maze of corridors with their many intersections on the first floor where the kitchen is located often becomes a haven for apparitions. Many times Justin has seen someone near the crossing of the corridors only to stop and look again. This time, they are not there. The length of the passageways would not permit anyone enough time to hide from plain sight.

The history of the structure is born of tragedy. John Winan, a Burlington ship builder, erected his home on the site in 1808. That year he began construction of Lake Champlain's first steamboat. In 1868, fire claimed the home but it was soon decided that the location was ideal for holding ice from the lake. An immense icehouse was soon rebuilt from the foundation to serve the region of the lake. Before the days of the electric refrigerator blocks of ice were used to keep perishable food cold in the warmer months. Men with special cutting tools and saws would venture out onto the frozen lakes and rivers and cut the ice into neat blocks. They would then haul the blocks of ice on horse drawn carriers to the specially insulated icehouses where they would be stacked for later use. Icehouses were still in use well into the twentieth century until the electric and gas refrigerators

The Ice House Restaurant is not only a place for great food, but it is haunted as well.
Photo courtesy of Victoria Julian.

became more popular and easier to obtain. In some places, icehouses still play an important role in the preserving of perishable goods. Milk trucks once not only used the ice to keep the dairy products cold while on delivery routes, they also supplied some of the homes with ice in the area I grew up in as late as the 1970s.

The massive three-story building supplied ice year round to the residents of Burlington for many generations with the chunks cut from Lake Champlain. It remained in operation well into the twentieth century before being converted into retail property.

The massive foot-square beams used to support the heavy ice still adorn the building as well as some entities from the past.

So, if you are in the area of Battery and King Streets in Burlington, Vermont, be sure to have a bite at the Ice House Restaurant. If you should feel a sudden cold chill while there, you'll know that it is not the ice doing its bid.

THE ICE HOUSE

Lake Champlain
Burlington, VT 05401

Take I-89 to Exit 14W and follow Main Street to Battery and King Streets along the docks. The restaurant is clearly marked.

The University of Vermont

My wife's daughter and her fiancé lived in Burlington very close to the University of Vermont. We often took the time to travel up to Burlington and stay the weekend visiting Mandy and Justin while taking in the sites. It was during one of those trips that I heard about the many spirits of the University of Vermont, or the UVM as it is more commonly known. UVM is Latin for Universitas Viridis Montis, the phrase that appears upon the official seal of the institution. It essentially means University of Green Mountains and was established in 1791, the same year Vermont became a state.

It was the fifth college to be established in New England behind Yale, Brown, Dartmouth, and Harvard. Many prominent people hailed from this institute of higher education like John McGill who was leader of Doctors Without Borders when it won the Noble Peace Prize in 1999, John Dewey, famous for the Dewey Decimal System, and Hollywood Producer John Kilik who is known for such movies as *Malcolm X, Dead Man Walking,* and *Do the Right Thing.* The list goes on and on.

We visited the campus on a Saturday in June and found it to be a very quaint educational facility, sprawling with history and of course, plenty of ghosts. Vermont author Joseph Citro investigated

Converse Hall's resident ghost, "Henry" likes
to play pranks on students and faculty alike.
Photo courtesy of Victoria Julian.

the university extensively and found no less than eleven buildings that were either haunted or had some sort of strange events taking place in them. We took a little tour of our own in the hope of meeting a few of the very old Vermonters from the other side of the veil.

The campus resembled a ghost town due to summer break but the spirits of the facility seem to still remain eternally enrolled in the school. Here are some of the more interesting haunts that presently remain notable at UVM.

Converse Hall

Converse Hall on South Prospect Street was erected in 1895. It served as a dorm for the students at that time. In the 1920s, a despondent medical student committed suicide in the building. Some say it was the pressure of keeping his grades up, while others claim he was a depressed individual with a weak sense of fortitude, thus making him unable to take on the rigors of medicine. Whatever the case, his spirit seems to have a lasting strength within the walls of Converse Hall.

The ghost is called Henry. Whether that was his real name or not is a matter of conjecture. Henry is known for opening and closing doors and windows throughout the building. He also enjoys playing with the lights at all hours of the day and night. Students and faculty have left a room only to see the glow of the lights suddenly emanate from the window or the crack at the bottom of the door.

There is a report of a ghostly typewriter that alarmed an undergraduate once. The student was alone in the room when the sound of typewriter keys began tapping. Upon investigation, all typewriter desks were vacant in the room. The thought of some ethereal fingers trying to communicate through the typewriter scared the student so much that she exited the room in frantic haste.

Furniture has a way of rearranging itself in empty rooms and small objects will suddenly take on wings and sail through the air with no visible hand to hurl them. Henry certainly keeps himself busy in Converse Hall but he is not the only phantom on campus. The others seem to be in eternal competition for attention in other buildings around UVM.

Counseling Center

Another building of reputed haunts is the Counseling Center located at South Williams and Main Street. Unlike Henry, who would rather stay unseen, the ghost in this old mansion is not afraid to show his presence. Some say it is the spirit of Captain John Nabb who built the mansion in the nineteenth century. Doors and windows also slam on their own and lights turn on and off. People have heard voices in the halls only to discover upon investigation, that they are the only mortal occupants of the corridors at that moment. Several reliable witnesses describe the ghost as a man with thick sideburns and a bulbous nose. He is known to have a bit of an angry streak to him, as the next account will relate. One custodian watched in disbelief as the spirit once passed by his cleaning bucket, overturning it onto the floor as he wisped down the hall. Maybe the captain is unhappy over the fate of his former home.

Old Mill

Old Mill is the university's oldest structure. It was rebuilt in 1824 after the original building was lost to a fire. People have experienced the sensation of being watched by unseen eyes. There is also ghostly activity on the second floor where the spirit of a lady has been seen in one of the rooms. No one is sure who she was though they think that she may have been a teacher at one time. The building was recently renovated so the spirit may have been activated by the changes in the Old Mill. Only time will tell.

Coolidge Hall Dormitory

The Coolidge Hall Dormitory has a few lingering alumni from the other side. One is the ghost of a young man who appears to residents during the dark hours of the night. Students have been stirred from their slumber only to find the wraith staring back at them.

Coolidge Hall has a few lingering alumni from the other side.
Photo courtesy of Victoria Julian.

Public Relations Building

The Public Relations Building has a ghost as well. The spirit is said to be former owner, John E. Booth. The Booth family owned the house from 1913 to 1967. Although he has stayed in the house, he is not much for the public relations thing. He has never been seen but his presence has been felt and he does play with lights. He also likes to hold doors closed on people as they try to open them. He makes noise around the house on occasion by banging into items or letting his voice be heard even if he would rather not be seen.

Wheeler House

Some of the spirits have faded with time. Take the Wheeler House for instance. The Reverend John Wheeler was the university's sixth president. It was reputed haunted by his daughter Lucia, who died in 1871 of tuberculosis (also known back then as consumption). Some witnesses have seen the ghost who they believe is Lucia while others have just heard her walking the halls at night when the house is otherwise empty. Over the years the haunting has dissipated to the point where her spirit is very rarely, if at all encountered within her former abode.

Former owner John E. Booth may be the spirit that is heard but not seen in this building now owned by UVM.
Photo courtesy of Victoria Julian.

Grasse Mount

Grasse Mount was a building I found to be historically interesting as well as paranormally tantalizing. The mansion, located at 411 Main Street was constructed in 1804 for Thaddeus Tuttle. He later sold it to Vermont Governor Cornelius Van Ness. It was the Governor's wife who named it Grasse Mount. He later sold it and after a few more transfers of deed, it came into the ownership of UVM in 1895. It now houses the Department of University Advancement as well as a few resident ghosts.

One time a former employee was closing up the building for the night when the windows began to rattle and the pipes and ducts of the heating system commenced to rumble and bang. This may not have seemed so out of the ordinary except that the system had been shut down for the summer to conserve unnecessary energy waste. The employee took the noises as a clue to make a quick departure from the old mansion.

Another employee experienced the entities of the manor in a different light. Late one evening, just around the witching hour, the whole place became a playground for mischievous spirits. Doors began to slam and footsteps were heard pounding up and down the halls. The windows and filing cabinet drawers rattled as if the earth itself was shaking. The frightened employee called security but there were no visible beings in the building to create the disturbance. Recent renovations to Grasse Mount have seemed to squelch the activity somewhat but people in the building still feel the daunting energy lurking in the shadows waiting for another unsuspecting person to be caught in their domain after the midnight hour.

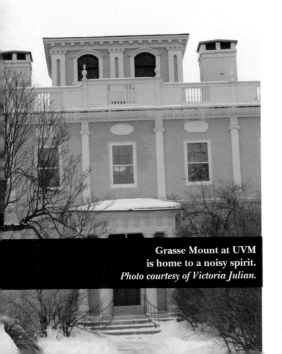

Grasse Mount at UVM is home to a noisy spirit.
Photo courtesy of Victoria Julian.

33

Bittersweet House

The most fascinating building we visited was the Bittersweet House located at the corner of South Prospect and Main Streets. This one I can say for sure harbors a ghost. When we arrived at the house, I wanted to go upstairs but it seems the secretary was a bit busy trying to catch up on her work. She told us that people always ask about the building and although she had heard strange noises around the house, she never witnessed any paranormal activity and did not believe in ghosts anyway. Fearing no chance of a tour, I asked to use the bathroom. I headed down the hall and up the stairs where I turned on my recorder to collect possible EVPs and began taking a few hasty pictures. I was hoping to capture an image of the most famous ghost on campus, Margaret L.H. Smith. The house was built in 1809 and is home to one of the most interesting accounts of all the haunted havens at UVM. This, of course, is my opinion, but read on and perhaps you too, will find in favor of my view.

It was named the Bittersweet House when Mrs. Smith's husband died in a car accident shortly after they bought the dream home. She stayed alone in the house right up until her death in 1961 at the age of ninety-four. She died in the house and many will swear that she still resides there in a now disembodied form. A few witnesses have seen the ghost of Margaret Smith walking through the halls dressed in a bell-shaped ankle-length skirt and a white high-collared blouse. Her hair is wrapped up neatly away from her neck. One employee of the building that is presently home to Environmental Programs has seen the spirit on several occasions.

The ghost of Margaret L.H. Smith still roams the halls of the Bittersweet House at UVM. Photo courtesy of Victoria Julian.

Others have seen her entity as more of a glowing form not as clearly defined in shape. Having a real ghost that appears frequently made this building the most intriguing of all the buildings on campus.

As I stood at the top of the stairs, I could feel the sensation one gets when there is more energy in a room than normal. I dismissed it as being excited about the day and that the Bittersweet House was our last stop. As I turned to leave, something caught my eye. It looked like the figure of a woman sliding quickly into one of the rooms down the small hall. I walked towards the room and attempted to get a better look inside, but the room was empty and the door was locked. Where, if there was another person upstairs with me, did she come from? I was at the top of the stairs and there was no way anyone could have gotten by me or come out of any other room without me seeing them.

I half concluded that it could have been my imagination wanting to see the ghost but I know what I felt and saw. My wife was thrilled over the fact that I may have witnessed a spirit at UVM.

Imagine my disappointment when all the pictures of the university for some strange reason, did not develop. The camera was in perfect working order as we always check our equipment before we use it. Also the tape recorder turned up no physical evidence of any paranormal activity. I am only left with the accounts I heard and have read about and what I may have witnessed in the Bittersweet

House as record of what many consider the university with the most college spirits.

American Flatbread Company

Many know this location as the former Carburs Restaurant. The establishment is a staple of Burlington and the paranormal realm in Vermont. The American Flatbread Company offers healthy fresh meals made from the finest organic ingredients. Their pizza is baked in a primitive wood fire oven. Their sauces are slow cooked thus making the cuisine offered at the restaurant a must try. There is also a bit of activity that seems to center in the basement of the restaurant.

Doors are known to slam shut, plates and glasses fly off the counters, and strange voices echo through the building when there is no physical being to orate the utterances. Waitresses have been trapped in the walk-in freezer or have had their skirts lifted by a sudden and mysterious cold wind. Activity is so frequent that the female staff has been advised not to venture into the basement anymore, as they seem to be the focal point of most of the paranormal activity. A bartender was cleaning up one evening and as part of her usual tasks, she washed all the drinking glasses and put them away. She turned to finish another chore and heard the tinkling sound of glasses banging against each other. When she whirled around towards the bar, the sight she beheld was most shocking. Sitting on top of the bar were the same glasses she had just put away stacked in a pyramid. The unnerving incident transpired within mere seconds of her walking away from the bar.

If it is delicious, natural food you crave, give the American Flatbread Company a try. It truly is a restaurant that is healthy in mind, body, and spirit.

AMERICAN FLATBREAD COMPANY

115 St. Paul Street
Burlington, VT 05401

Take Exit 14W US-2 toward Burlington off I-89 and follow into downtown. Take a right onto St. Paul Street.

Merchant's Bank

This small building used to be the office of an attorney who stayed on to practice law long after he was well suited for retirement. The Merchant's Bank now occupies on the premises but they share it with a ghost. The apparition of an old man is often seen sitting in the employee lounge by staff as they enter the room. The visage then steadfastly vanishes before them. Who is the aged spirit? Employees seem to think it is the ghost of the lawyer who once practiced in the building, as the lounge was once his office. Customers of the bank must feel good that there is always one entity permanently residing in the building watching their money.

THE MERCHANT'S BANK

164 College Street
Burlington, VT 05401

Take Exit 14W, US-2 off of I-89. Take a right onto St. Paul Street and another right onto College Street.

CALAIS

They Freeze Them, Don't They?

This next tale is one I have heard since I was a child. My grandfather on my mother's side was raised in Swanton, just south of the Canadian border. It was a matter of course that I would learn much about the legends and tales of Vermont. I owe special thanks to Joseph Citro for bringing me the story as it first appeared in the Montpelier *Argus and Patriot* on December 21, 1887. This version also appears in his book, *Green Mountains, Dark Tales*. He also discovered the full name of the writer of this grim narrative. For decades, all the reader had as credit for the story had been two initials; A.M. Without further ado, I shall let you the reader, peruse this weird gem and then later give you a bit more particulars on this legend.

A Strange Tale

By Allen Morse

I am an old man now, and have seen some strange sights in the course of a roving life in foreign lands as well as in this country, but none so strange as one I found recorded in an old diary, kept by my Uncle William, that came into my possession a few years ago, at his decease. The events described took place in a mountain town some twenty miles from Montpelier, the Capital of Vermont. I have been to the place on the mountain, and seen the old log-house where the events I found recorded in the diary took place, and seen and talked with an old man who vouched for the truth of the story, and that his father was one of the parties operated on. The account runs in this wise:

"*January 7*—I went on the mountain today, and witnessed what to me was a horrible sight. It seems that the dwellers there, who are unable, either from age or other reasons, to contribute to the support of their families, are disposed of in the winter months in a manner that will shock the one who reads this diary, unless that person lives in that vicinity. I will describe what I saw. Six persons, four men and two women, one of the men a cripple about 30 years old, the other five past the age of usefulness, lay on the earthy floor of the cabin drugged into insensibility, while members of their families were gathered about them in apparent indifference. In a short time the unconscious bodies were inspected by one man who said, "They are ready." They were then stripped of all their clothing, except a single garment. Then the bodies were carried outside, and laid on logs exposed to the bitter cold mountain air, the operation having been delayed several days for suitable weather.

"It was night when the bodies were carried out, and the full moon, occasionally obscured by flying clouds, shone on their upturned ghastly faces, and a horrible fascination kept me by the bodies as long as I could endure the severe cold. Soon the noses, ears and fingers began to turn white, then the limbs and face assumed a tallowy look. I could stand the cold no longer, and went inside, where I found the friends in cheerful conversation.

"In about an hour I went out and looked at the bodies: they were fast freezing. Again I went inside, where the men were smoking their clay pipes, but silence had fallen on them; perhaps they were thinking of the time when their turn would come to be cared for in the same way. One by one they at last lay down on the floor, and went to sleep. It seemed a horrible nightmare to me, and I could not think of sleep. I could not shut out the sight of those freezing bodies outside, neither could I bear to be in darkness, but I piled on the wood in the cavernous fireplace, and, seated on a shingle block, passed the dreary night, terror-stricken by the horrible sights I had witnessed.

"*January 8*—Day came at length, but did not dissipate the terror that filled me. The frozen bodies became visible, white as the snow that lay in huge drifts about them. The women gathered about the fire, and soon commenced preparing breakfast. The men awoke, and, conversation again commencing, affairs assumed a more cheerful aspect. After breakfast the men lighted their pipes, and some of them took a yoke of oxen and went off toward the forest, while others proceeded to nail together boards, making a box about ten feet long and half as high and wide. When this was completed they placed about two feet of straw in the bottom; then they laid three of the frozen bodies on the straw. Then the faces and upper part of the bodies were covered with a cloth, then more straw was put in the box, and the other three bodies placed on top and covered the same as the first ones, with cloth and straw. Boards were then firmly nailed on the top, to protect the bodies from being injured by carnivorous animals that make their home on these mountains.

"By this time the men who went off with the ox-team returned with a huge load of spruce and hemlock boughs, which they unloaded at the foot of a steep ledge, came to the house and loaded the box containing the bodies on the sled, and drew it to the foot of the ledge, near the load of boughs. These were soon piled on and around the box, and it was left to be covered up with snow, which I was told would lie in drifts twenty feet deep over this rude tomb. 'We shall want our men to plant our corn next spring,' said a youngish looking woman, the wife of one of the frozen men, 'and if you want to see them resuscitated, you come here about the 10th of next May.'

"With this agreement, I left the mountaineers, both the living and the frozen, to their fate and I returned to my home in Boston where it was weeks before I was fairly myself, as my thoughts would return to that mountain with its awful sepulcher." Turning the leaves of the diary to the date of May 10, the following entry was found:

"*May 10*—I arrived here at 10 AM, after riding about four hours over muddy, unsettled roads. The weather is warm and pleasant, most of the snow is gone, except here and there drifts in the fence corners and hollows, but nature is not yet dressed in green. I found the same parties here that I left last January, ready to disinter the bodies of their friends. I had no expectation of finding any life there, but a feeling that I could not resist impelled me to come and see. We repaired at once to the well remembered spot, at the ledge. The snow had melted from the top of the brush, but still lay deep around the bottom of the pile. The men commenced work at once, some shoveling away the snow, and others tearing away the brush. Soon the box was visible. The cover was taken off, the layers of straw removed, and the bodies, frozen and apparently lifeless, lifted out and laid on the snow.

Large troughs made out of hemlock logs were placed nearby, filled with tepid water, into which the bodies were separately placed, with the head slightly raised. Boiling water was then poured into the trough from kettles hung on poles over fires near by, until the water in the trough was as hot as I could hold my hand in. Hemlock boughs had been put in the boiling water in such quantities that they had given the water the color of wine. After lying in this bath about an hour, color began to return to the bodies, when all hands began rubbing and chafing them. This continued about another hour, when a slight twitching of the muscles of the face and limbs, followed by audible gasps, showed that life was not quenched, and that vitality was returning. Spirits were then given in small quantities, and allowed to trickle down their throats. Soon they could swallow, and more was given them, when their eyes opened, and they began to talk, and finally sat up in their bath-tubs. They were then taken out and assisted to the house, where after a hearty dinner they seemed as well as ever, and in nowise injured, but rather refreshed, by their long sleep of four months."

So, there you have it. Believable? To many, yes. Science has proven that we can freeze animate objects and later on restore them after thawing. Were these Vermonters ahead of their time or was Mr. Morse a grand teller of tales? Allen Morse was a dairy farmer from Calais. He was born in 1835 and died in 1917. He was known to be the king of "yarnin." When the old folks got together to tell stories, the next would have to top the previous. It was entertaining in those days to wile away the hours by a country store wood stove and spin fantastic "true" accounts they had witnessed in their lives. How much was actually true? That is the real mysterious part of this tale.

For what it is worth, *The Rutland Herald* and *Boston Globe* printed the story in 1939. It was then picked up by *Yankee* magazine. Many other periodicals and books would follow. Even *The Old Farmer's Almanac* brought eventual worldwide exposure to the

Photo Courtesy of John DaSilva.

accounts "witnessed" by Mr. A.M. So it is time to ask, what do you believe? No matter what you may answer, there are many out there who have no doubt that this strange custom came out of the cabin closet in 1887. Perhaps it was just a yarn, perhaps a lot more…

CALAIS

North of Montpelier

Take Route I-89 to Exit 8, Route 12. Follow Route 12 North to Worcester and look for signs to Maple Corner, Kent's Corner or East Calais. The P.O. box for Calais is Maple Corner.

CASTLETON

Lake Bomoseen

The little settlement and quarries of West Castleton now lie silent and abandoned but there was a time when the sounds of steady labor and life buzzed through this little corner of the town, echoing across Lake Bomoseen. The West Castleton Railroad and Slate Company once thrived near the shores of the lake. The company had sixty to seventy buildings scattered about the perimeter, but now all that remains are several remnants in the form of foundations and crumbling edifices of an era long past. The quarries are presently part of Bomoseen State Park, a 3,576-acre wilderness getaway located in the Taconic Mountains along the shore of the lake. The Slate History Trail is a three-quarter mile trail that takes adventurers through the remains of the old slate company.

Legend holds that Irish immigrants found work in the quarries and lived in the homes nearby. For entertainment, many would row across to the eastern side of the lake to partake in some libations and laughter at the local tavern. One night, three men set out in a rowboat across the lake to the watering hole. Somewhere along the way, they disappeared, never to be seen or heard from again. The next morning, the dory was found floating with no one on board.

Now residents and visitors of the lake often spy a phantom rowboat slowly and silently moving across the lake with no one aboard. The vessel creates not a single ripple nor sound as it seems to glide along the calm glassy surface reflected by the gibbous moon.

If you are more than curious and would like to test the legend yourself, the park offers sixty-six campsites with ten lean-tos along the lake. Who knows? You might be camping along the shore when the three men decide to finally come back.

LAKE BOMOSEEN STATE PARK

1422 West Castleton Road
Castleton, VT 05735

Take Exit 6 off of I-91 for US-5 toward Rutland/VT-103/Rockingham. Turn left at Rockingham Road/ US-5. Continue onto VT-103. Take a right onto Route 7B. Turn right onto Ethan Allen Highway then left onto US-4 West. Take Exit 3, VT-4A. Turn right onto Scotch Hill Road. Take left onto Moscow Road and then first left onto Glen Lake Road. Look for state park.

CAVENDISH

The Mysterious Deacon Wheelock's Farmhouse

There are times when a story holds a bit more than what can be read on the surface. As we dig deeper for the truth, we find a bizarre twist that had been forgotten in the annals of time. These accounts are long forgotten, yet are no less macabre than the legends that precede them. As the shadows on your wall grow tall and thin with the waning daylight, try to remember that the opening segment of this next account may not be totally substantiated. It is the other story, the second part of this narrative, meticulously uncovered by research that may really make you think in bewilderment of the Yankee disposition of centuries past.

Deacon Jonathon Wheelock reportedly built his home in Cavendish around 1789. He also founded the first Episcopalian church in town. It is written that he was a victim of a violent accident and subsequently died from his injuries. The home now reportedly sustains ghost and poltergeist activity by an unidentified restless spirit or two. According to sources, items disappear from one place and are found in another spot that is not in common with where they should be. Plates, knick-knacks, and other such pieces suddenly take on wings and fly off of shelves, crashing to the floor. Then there are the apparitions that appear in front of wide-eyed witnesses. Some claim to have awoken in the dark hours of the night only to spy a bluish form staring back at them. Others have seen the same presence looking out a window.

Such legends prompted Arlene and I to find this house. With the gracious help of historians Linda Welch and Margaret Caulfield, we were able to find out more than we bargained for about the Wheelock homestead. Linda Welch published a few books for the Cavendish Historical Society. They are quite interesting and thorough. The book, *Families of Cavendish*, tells a bit more of the story.

Jotham Wheelock was born to Deacon Johnathon and Ann Drury Wheelock on August 26, 1763. He was a sergeant in the sixth Continental Line under Captain Daniels Co., Sixth Massachusetts Regulars until 1780. He then removed to Cavendish to join his parents. Somewhere in between he had a son, Jotham Jr. According to town records and the Historical Society's book called, *Heritage and Homes of Cavendish*, Jotham Sr. deeded his property to his son in 1793 along with fifty acres across the road. It is listed in the book as the Sanders Farm. According to Margaret Caulfield, the farm was handed down to a number of people over the years and is at present, the property of Mildred and Eddy Fitzgibbons. Margaret actually called the couple in relation to the ghosts but they stated that they never encountered any strange activity while there. (They did state that the current house they live in is haunted though.)

This brings us back to the ghost story associated with the house. Jotham was stricken with a disease or head injury during his service in the Revolutionary War. This left him a bit mentally unstable. The illness got worse until his family had to take care of him with the pension he received from his military service. Before he died, he strongly demanded that a heavy plank filled with long spikes be placed just above his coffin. He was afraid that the devil would attempt to rob the grave of his corpse and carry him to hell.

Jotham died in Cavendish on April 27, 1831. He was buried on the road between the Morgan place and the Sanders place. The grave is about halfway between the two farms. Col. Wilgus, a descendant of the Wheelocks had a granite marker set at the site of his grave. And yes, he was buried with the plank full of spikes.

As for the ghosts, perhaps they are there, perhaps not. If so, could it be the deacon still at unrest over his untimely demise? Maybe Jotham is resting peacefully under his protective pin cushion quite possibly, the job was not done as well as he thought it might be and he now roams the area trying to hide from the evil one of whom he was sure would take him to the underworld. Far fetched? Remember, this is New England, namely Vermont where truth is often stranger than fiction.

The Bowman Mausoleum.
Photo courtesy of Victoria Julian.

CUTTINGSVILLE

Bowman Mansion

As one drives down Route 103 in Cuttingsville, an eerie sight unexpectedly looms before them. It is the mournful figure of a man crouching along side the door of the Laurel Glen Mausoleum with a wreath in one hand and a top hat in the other. It is not a ghostly apparition but rather a stone figure of John Porter Bowman, a wealthy farmer and tanning tycoon who had the crypt erected for his beloved family.

Since 1881, the statue has graced the steps of the vault, ten years before Mr. Bowman himself passed away. One hundred and twenty-five masons and sculptors worked for a little over a year to complete the bizarre structure. Inside lie the remains of the Bowman family, a stone bust of both his wife, Jenny, and daughter, Ella, who died tragically and mysteriously within several months of each other. A life-size statue of his first daughter, Addie, who died as an infant stands on one side, and the bust of John P. Bowman, who passed away in 1891, faces all of them.

The reason behind the granite likeness of him waiting outside the door of the vault, gently poised as if ready to hear the sounds of his family once again remains a mystery. The strange mausoleum is reported haunted by the voices of the Bowman family. If that is the case, then they do not spend much time there for across the street is the Bowman Mansion and it is definitely alive with the ghosts of the family.

The Bowman House is now a museum offering tours of the beautiful historical building. Clarendon native John P. Bowman supposedly built the great home for his wife and family after making his fortune in tanning. Some historical records indicate that his wife was already deceased when he built the structure they had dreamed of together in life. Either way, his family died suddenly and mysteriously. Their first child, Addie, died in 1854. She was only an infant at the time of her death. Ella was twenty-two years old when she passed away in 1879. His wife Jenny followed shortly after in 1880. Some say it was one of the dreaded diseases of the time.

The Bowman House and Museum.
Photo courtesy of Victoria Julian.

Consumption, now known as tuberculosis, was a horrible illness of which there was no cure. The malady wiped out whole families without compassion. Other sicknesses such as typhoid or scarlet fever were also quite terminal and contagious at that time. Others say it could have been a series of strange accidents that claimed the lives of his family. No one really knows what happened but it left Mr. Bowman a widower without children.

Mr. Bowman would live about ten years in his grief before joining them in death. When he passed away, he set up a trust fund for the upkeep of the mansion and grounds. Today the site is a historical landmark and visitors are immediately transported back to the 1800s when the house crowed in the era of its most flourishing moments. There is another side of the mansion that makes it a bit darker in nature; the ghosts that reside within.

One such haunt is the apparition of an unknown woman that has been witnessed throughout the mansion. Many think it is the spirit of Mrs. Bowman still going about her daily routine over 120 years after her death. Witnesses have seen her cleaning and tidying up some of the rooms. Sometimes she is seen walking through the rooms and vanishing into thin air. Perhaps her spirit has traversed over to the mansion from the cemetery across the street to eternally reside in the home she wanted in life.

There is a peculiar dark stain at the top of the staircase of unknown origin. Some think it is a bloodstain that has something to do with the sudden and tragic deaths of Mr. Bowman's family. Whatever the case, visitors of the house get a frightening, negative feeling of dread when they stand in that spot. Psychics have been frightened out of the house by the stain and the horrible feeling they experienced when coming in contact with the mysterious blot.

A little girl who was touring the house with her parents did not particularly care for a certain picture she saw on the wall overlooking the staircase. To show her disapproval of the portrait, she stuck her tongue out at it. The picture flew off of the wall and struck the little girl right in front of the whole tour group and guide. It appears that the ghosts of the house do not tolerate unruly behavior in their abode. It appears that they do not tolerate guests after the sun has gone down as well. No one is allowed to stay in the house after dark. Some people have tried to occupy the residence but the spirits were so noisy and intrusive that they were forced to leave the house altogether.

There is also a haunted house book shop on the grounds of the mansion that is open for visitors to peruse. After dark however, that must also be vacated and left to the spirits of the mansion to catch up on some ethereal reading, or in their case, stories of their world.

THE BOWMAN MANSION AND CEMETERY

Route 103 just southeast
of Rutland, VT

Take Interstate I-91 into Central
Vermont. Take Exit 6, Route 103
into Cuttingsville.

DORSET

Dorset Inn

Dorset is your quintessential Vermont village complete with a green, shops, and a few inns where travelers can stay a night or two and relish in the atmosphere of the little hamlet. The Dorset Inn just happens to be one of those lovely places to stay while in town. Since 1796, the Dorset Inn has welcomed travelers on their journey to places such as Boston, Massachusetts, and Albany, New York. The inn became a popular stop for many to partake in some food, froth, and fresh beds.

The elegant Dorset Inn has a few permanent guests that make an appearance now and then.
Photo courtesy of Victoria Julian.

In 1918, the roof over the ballroom was raised to accommodate more guests to the growing inn. When chef Sissy Hicks took over the inn in 1985, it was renovated with care as to not remove or destroy any of the original appointments and details of the historic building. Present innkeepers, Steve and Lauren Bryant recently became the latest owners of the Dorset Inn with the undertaking of keeping the inn's ageless charm and splendor untouched.

There are plenty of beautifully decorated guest rooms; several being part of the original structure where guests can enjoy the views of Vermont's picturesque countryside. The Dorset is also renowned for its fabulous cuisine. The *Wine Spectator* voted the establishment as one of America's best restaurants in 2008. Diners can enjoy fine fare in either the historic red dining room or the on-site tavern. They may have the opportunity to meet the oldest guest of the inn—a ghost the staff affectionately calls "The General."

The general has been seen by staff and guests alike. He is dressed in a dark military uniform with gold braid, much like the uniforms of the Civil War. According to members of the Dorset staff, he is often seen in the taproom. One employee also witnessed him roaming the third floor for a short time. He has also been accompanied on occasion by the visage of a woman in an old-fashioned long skirt and a child. No one knows when he is going to make his appearance and his exact identity is lost to

antiquity, but he still likes to make a showing now and then.

Our friends, Robert Hughes and Victoria Julian stayed at the Dorset Inn during their last tour of Vermont. Being avid paranormal enthusiasts and investigators, it was natural for them to want to investigate the premises during their visit. Steve let them do a vigil or two around the building, and even showed them the cellar, which was reported to be a part of the Underground Railroad.

During their investigations, they collected a few interesting pieces of evidence. One is what appears to be a bluish orb moving across the basement and the others are a few EVPs. The EVP session took place in Room 35, a place where the general is also reported to visit from time to time. Among the several questions asked during a particular EVP session, Vickie politely inquired, "How old are you?" The answer was very audible and sounded like, "Ten." At that point, the lights on the K-II meter lit up and stayed lit. Here is what happened over the next few minutes while the lights on the meter stayed lit.

She then asked more questions.

"What season is it?"

No answer.

"Are you here by yourself?"

Silence again.

"Are you a female?"

There is a faint but audible "No."

"Are you a male?"

No answer.

"Do you like visitors?"

"Where did you come from?"

Possible orb in the basement of the Dorset Inn.
Photo courtesy of Victoria Julian.

After that question there is a faint answer that sounds like "Here." Perhaps the spirit was relating that it came from either the inn or the village.

"Where are you traveling to?"

"Did you ride a horse to get here?"

"How old are You?"

Once again a voice, this time a bit fainter than before answers, "Ten."

"Do you like us being here with you?"

"Do you want us to come back and visit?"

"Is there anything we can help you with?"

At that point, the lights on the meter went down and all was quiet.

Vickie then thanked the spirits for taking the time to converse with her and was eager to hear what they had to say, but listening to the recorder for EVPs would have to wait until after the investigation was completed.

The rest of the investigation was quiet, but it appears that they may have contacted the spirit of the child that sometimes accompanies the general. Perhaps it is another spirit altogether. With a place that is over 200 years old, it can be assured that there is a lot of energy lingering within. But, do not worry; all of it is friendly and positive. That is why the Dorset Inn is such a wonderful place to visit and stay; it has the endorsement of some permanent guests. If they are not in a hurry to leave, then it must be a nice place to relax, at least for an evening or two while basking in the history and hospitality the inn has to offer.

THE DORSET INN

8 Church Street On the Green, Dorset, VT 05251
(802) 867-5500

Take I-91 North to Brattleboro exits 1 or 2 to Route 30 North. Follow Route 30 North through Manchester to Dorset Village.

IN MEMORY OF
CAPT. JOHN KATHAN
CAME TO N. E. IN 1729
FIRST SETTLER OF DUMMERSTON
LOCATING
S. E. OF PUTNEY R. R. STATION
JUNE 5, 1752
DIED NOV. 23, 1787
Æ. 81 YRS.

MARTHA MOORE HIS WIFE
DIED SEPT. 22, 1766
Æ. 62 YRS.

BOTH BURIED
IN KATHAN CEMETERY PUTNEY
ERECTED BY DESCENDENTS
OF THE SIXTH GENERATION

First settler of Dummerston

DUMMERSTON

Among the Undead

One of the First Recorded
New England Vampire Cases

Many people still wonder in awe about the legends of the New England vampires. Even more noteworthy, is the difference in the beliefs from state to state and the class difference between the different locales. On the one side, you have the rural farmers of Rhode Island who, in some cases had not yet discovered that the actual cause of their affliction from beyond the grave was treatable not more than twenty miles away from their pastures. On the other side there are the Vermont vampire cases. The families recorded in these following accounts were intelligent, well-bred people, some founding fathers of their towns. Yet, they embraced the notion of the undead that gripped them with fear, causing them to defy all rational thought and reasoning. Their dilemma led them to espouse strange beliefs and superstitions even the backwoods folk of the Ocean State

would never consider as a possible symptom that took their families to an early grave. Read on and let this account, one of the first recorded cases of vampirism in New England, be the threshold to a world where superstition and strange cures for what they truly believed was the work of the undead, became very real. If all the dates are correct, this case took place in early 1793, just about the same time Isaac Burton of Manchester was having his own dilemma with the supernatural.

Of course, the term "vampire" was probably not used then, at least not in the outspoken respect. It was more than likely whispered within the secluded corners of the village store or tavern or kept within the panes of the homes afflicted with the dreaded sickness then called consumption. The word vampire made its way into the *Oxford English Dictionary* in 1734. From there it seems to have been introduced to the colonies when the *Hartford Courant* reprinted the dictionary in 1765 with the word and definition of "vampyre."

Lieutenant Leonard Spaulding was a celebrated war hero and first representative to the Vermont Legislature. In 1756, he married Margaret Sprague Love of Providence, Rhode Island. He served at Crown Point in 1758. He fought in the French and Indian War, and later, the American Revolution. In 1756, he married Margaret Sprague Love of Providence, Rhode Island. He served at Crown Point in 1758. Spaulding later settled in Putney around 1768. His house burned in 1771 and from there, he moved to a farm in Westmoreland, New Hampshire. He remained there less than one year before removing himself and his family to Dummerston. He was wounded in the skirmish at Westminster on March 13, 1775 but this did not stop him in his cause for the freedom of the colonies from British rule. While

Lt. Spaulding's marker in Burnett Cemetery just west of Route 5 in Dummerston.

he fought the revolution, his wife and sons, Reuben and Leonard Jr., tended to the farm. During the Battle of Bennington in 1777, it is reported that Spaulding's wife was in the garden picking vegetables for dinner when she heard the distant roar of cannons. Others had heard the noise as well but construed it to be thunder from afar. No one was aware of the famous battle that raged but forty miles from the Spaulding homestead until later. It was also a surprise when the family later found out that Spaulding was fighting in that battle as well.

Lt. Spaulding represented Dummerston in the General Assembly in 1778, 1781, 1784, 1786, and 1787. He is quite a notable figure in the history of Vermont. There is another history that he is also noted for, the dark legends of vampires that once roamed the countryside of New England. It seemed that fame or prominence held no credence in regard to the curse of the vampire. Several of his children died of consumption at a young age. Mary died on May 12, 1782 at the age of 20 years. Sarah died on October 27 of the same year at the age of 19. Esther followed them in July of 1783 at the age of 16. Lt. Spaulding was the next to succumb to the wasting disease. On July 17, 1788, he died at the age of 59. As per request, Lt. Spaulding was buried in a graveyard east of what is presently known as Slab Hollow. The burial ground is known as Burnett Cemetery just west of Route 5 and Schoolhouse Road. This was due to the fact that the resting place of his children

had turned into a bog and burial was out of the question. There is a marker to his memorial at the far end of the aforementioned burial yard.

It was less than two years after his death that thirty-one year old Betsey followed her father and brothers to the grave. Then it was thirty-two-year-old Leonard Jr.'s turn on September 3, 1792. This is the death that suggested a demonic force was at work. Some scholars state that it was John Spaulding, twin brother to Timothy, who sparked the vampire notion with his death on March 26, 1793. (There are claims that it may have been Josiah several years later but, as before, no exact names have been penned in regard to what sibling was the actual catalyst that sparked the need for the exorcism.)

Around this time, another of the Spaulding daughters became ill with the same disease. There was now talk of a much needed exorcism. The Spaulding boys were all very healthy, large in stature, and strong, yet succumbed to the wasting illness quite rapidly and without much of a chance of survival. All but two died under forty years of age. The townsfolk, although not outwardly uttering the word vampire, knew what was taking the family one by one to their eternal rest. The locals seemed utterly convinced that there was a hungry spirit of the undead among them.

There was also a strange superstition that reared its head at this time. It was claimed that if a vine or root grew from one coffin to the next of the family members who died of consumption, and were buried side by side, when the vine reached the coffin of the last to be interred, another would soon die. The only way to overcome the curse was to break the vine, dig up the body of the last one buried, and burn the vitals. Hence the vine was cut, the last Spaulding to be interred was dug up, and the vitals were cut out of the body. They in turn were burned. The daughter, strangely enough, recovered from her malady and went on to live a long healthy life. It does not state the daughter, but we can guess that it may have been Anna, who died January 13, 1849 at the age of eighty-one years, nine months, and six days. Reuben and Josiah both died young as well. Reuben, on January 20, 1794 at the age of twenty-eight years and Josiah on December 3, 1798 at the age of twenty-seven. Margaret Spaulding lived to be ninety-four. She died May 21, 1827 and is buried next to Anna although there is no stone marking her plot.

One of the most compelling pieces of evidence in this case that suggests, as far as I am concerned, that it might be Vermont's first recorded case, is the aspect of the vine. In no other cases that follow does such a remedial ceremony take place. It does however, first show up in a 1784 writing from Willington, Connecticut, where it is mentioned that a foreign doctor prescribed such remedial steps to stop the demise of members from the family of Isaac Johnson. Perhaps in the cases that followed there was no vine or root growing across the coffins, or they were not buried exactly side by side. There was, however a recently interred loved one that when dug up, was a bit more suspect than the others. This would lend to the notion of quickly dropping the vine theory but keeping the vampire one as later cases had the same protocol in removing the vitals and burning them. If this had happened as a later example, chances are they would not have used the vine as a catalyst in their plight. Then again, we know little about the actual fear and feelings they had concerning the fact that one of their own might have been a spectral ghoul rising from the grave in the dark bowers of the night to feed upon their own flesh and blood. Lets continue our tour of the ghosts and other strange phenomena that Vermont holds.

ENOSBURG FALLS

Enosburg Opera House

Just seven miles from the Canadian border, Enosburg Falls is definitely a Northern New England community. It was named after General Roger Enos. The small village is typical of the wondrous charming hamlets seen throughout New England. It also boasts another aspect that is seen throughout the region—hauntings. One such place is the Enosburg Opera House. Dr. B.J. Kendall built the opera house in 1892 at the cost of ten thousand dollars. It featured both local and traveling entertainment until the 1950s. It also doubled as a place for town meetings and large school events.

Soon, a school gymnasium was erected. This, along with outdoor tourist activities and the advent of the television, left the opera house empty and decaying. It began to deteriorate quickly until a group called the Enosburg Opera House Association came to the rescue and gave the building a face-lift and new purpose. In 1993, full restoration was under way thanks to the help of the Vermont Historic Preservation Trust and architect Roland Batten. They all formed what is now called, Friends of the Opera House. The opera house once again glimmers with stage lights and hosts a wide variety of venues that are sure to please everyone. It also seems to host a spirit or two.

A man named Henry, (sometimes called Willy) fell while working in the attic. He broke his leg quite badly and was unable to drag himself to any kind of aid. No one came around for days to check on the building so he was stranded up there where he eventually died from his injuries. Henry's ghost seems to keep well hidden from the eyes of the living, although he does have a way of making his presence known in many mischievous ways.

Henry likes to move props and steal playbooks. Even the renovations of the opera house failed to jostle Henry from his eternal feistiness. Both patrons and staff alike hear phantom footsteps in the otherwise empty attic on a regular basis. Jon Scott was Executive

Director of the non-profit society that runs the opera house. He has heard Henry puttering around on many occasions when he was certain that there was no one else in the building other than himself.

Henry does not roam the entire building, however. He has never been known to haunt the ground floor of the opera house. He keeps his haunts confined to the second-floor stage, hall, and attic. Perhaps the hustle and bustle of the ground floor, where the entrance and ticket booths are located, can become a bit too much for the shy ghost. He does keep rather quiet during performances suggesting that he might be a bit of a connoisseur of the performing arts. His spirit is not malevolent by any means—he just wants to be noticed. Maybe even to land a part in one of the plays. Whatever the case may be, it is probably safe to say that the term "break a leg" is not used very often at the Enosburg Opera House.

ENOSBURG OPERA HOUSE

Village of Enosburg Falls

Take Interstate 89 to Exit 19, VT-104 toward VT-36/US-7/St. Albans. Merge onto St. Albans Street-South. Bear right onto VT-104 then right onto VT-105 into Enosburg Falls.

FAIRLEE

Lake Morey

History and haunts seem to go hand in hand. Perhaps it is the particular historical content of the event that creates the haunting to begin with or maybe it is just a moment in time replaying itself through a residual haunt that happens to have some sort of exciting historical significance. Residual haunts are not intelligent haunts or ghosts; they are a moment in time that has been recorded or taped somehow by the earth much like a DVD or CD and replayed at random. There are many theories as to how this happens. Famous author and researcher Paul Eno has studied and applied the laws of quantum physics to many cases where this occurrence has been prevalent. His theories and findings have helped propel the paranormal field into a higher level of scientific approach, one definitely worth studying. In the case of Lake Morey, history seems to be mixed with a very strange haunt that could be more than just a residual—possibly a powerful recant of

one's anger over the feeling that his idea may have been, according to his purports, stolen.

Samuel Morey (October 23, 1762 – April 17, 1843) patented several inventions that involved the steam engine. One of them was a steamboat. Between 1790 and 1793, he worked on his invention with full enthusiasm. On a Sunday in 1792, he made the first successful steamboat run in one of his inventions, a waterwheel steamboat with the wheel situated in the prow of the vessel. Legend says that he chose Sunday morning because the townsfolk were all in church; this way he could avoid embarrassment should the voyage result in failure. His several mile run at an astounding four miles an hour on the Connecticut River was sure to usher in a new age of transportation. He built three known boats during his experiments.

By 1797, Morey considered his boat ready for commercial use and sought financial backers. Backing for his boat fell through due to a series of misfortunes so he turned away from steam power and began working and experimenting more in the field of internal combustion. He did make more improvements on the steam engine as evident in his 1799, 1800, and 1803 patents.

In the meantime, a man named Robert Fulton was also very interested in the steamboat and in 1807, launched the first commercial passenger steamer, which ran from New York to Albany. When Fulton and his financier, Chancellor Robert Livingston were hailed as the inventors of the steamboat, Morey was a bit outraged, claiming that they took some of his ideas to create their boat. There is record of Livingston riding on Morey's steamboat a few years before. Morey also rode on Fulton's boat and made it known he was not happy that Fulton reaped the benefits of his hard work.

According to local legend, Morey was so disgusted with the situation that he took his boat, the *Aunt Sally* to the middle of the lake and sank it. The lake was later named in his honor, as he resided in Fairlee until his death in 1843. He is buried in Orford, New Hampshire, but that has not kept his spirit from wandering to his former home.

It is recanted among the citizens of this quaint town that when the moon shines bright upon the earth, the calm plane of the lake is disrupted by the rising of the *Aunt Sally*. The phantom vessel then floats across the lake creating no sound or ripple in its wake. Even more eerie, is the visage of a figure that is spied watching the ghostly craft from the shore. It is none other than the countenance of Captain Samuel Morey himself summoning up his steamer to once again roll along the waters of the haunted lake. If you decide to stay a while in hopes of seeing the captain and his boat, you might be able to witness it from the Lake Morey Resort.

LAKE MOREY

Fairlee, VT 05045

The resort is located on the lake. To get there take Exit 15 off of I-91 (left off exit from the south right from the north) and take first right at sign that says, "Granite Lake Morey Resort;" then take first left onto Clubhouse Road to resort. Other areas and information about the lake can be procured there.

GLASTENBURY

Glastenbury / Long Trail

Some people believe that there are entrances or gates that lead back and forth to places far removed from our plane of existence. They exist in a warp in time or a wormhole. Perhaps they are the thin veils between dimensions. Glastenbury, Vermont quite possibly may have such an enigma of physics hovering in the woods, waiting for the unsuspecting hiker to carelessly meander into. Sounds like something out of a science fiction novel? As you read on, you will find this bizarre declaration a bit more palatable. But, that is not the only evil that lurks among the now-defunct ghost town. Hold close to your senses, and be alert of those noises that wane in the background as you read on. They might hold the secrets that no one has ever been able to tell of the cursed mountain village.

But first, lets get a little history of what is now but cellar holes and crumbling ruins along the Long Trail in Vermont. On August 20, 1761, Benning Wentworth, then Governor of the Province of New Hampshire, charted out the territory of what would later become Vermont. He cut the areas in squares. He then named a square after himself. This would become Bennington, of course. The area near it he named Glastonbury. A few days later he named its neighbor Somerset. These were in honor of Glastonbury, Somerset, England. Along the way, Glastonbury became Glastenbury. Early settlers came from Rhode Island. They were the Mattisons and the Hazards. Life was tough there but the few families were not afraid to brave the rigors of the territory. Then there was the curse.

It is not completely known if the settlers knew of the so-called curse. The Native Indians of the area avoided the mountain, swearing that evil creatures inhabited it. These creatures were known to bring death and destruction to those who trespassed upon their soil. When Vermont became a state in 1791, there were thirty-four people living in the Glastenbury settlement. It did not become an official town until 1834. At that point, it had fifty residents. Maybe the curse waited for the village to become an official place on the map. Shortly after its inception into Vermont's books, children began dying of whooping cough and mothers strangely succumbed to death during childbirth. One family lost six children to diphtheria. One day, a resident from town wandered down river to do some fishing and was never seen or heard from again. Search parties scoured the area in vain looking for the man who had seemingly vanished from the face of the earth. Some time after he disappeared, a skull was found on a stump near the area where he had vanished.

Other strange stories of giant creatures began to pervade the tense mountain air of the village. There is one report from a newspaper during the nineteenth century where a stagecoach traveling the Glastenbury Plank Road suddenly stopped when the horses reared and bucked. The driver, thinking it was a bobcat or wolf, fetched his rifle and jumped from the reins to shoo the pesky creature away. As he looked down, he became startled by the gargantuan set of animal tracks in the mud just beside him. He called to the passengers who alit from the coach to behold the eerie prints. As they stared at the impressions, the horses let out a frightened whinny and leaped in terror. In an instant, something slammed into the side of the coach sending it roof over end. A giant inhuman creature then glared

back at the terrified throng with "great glinting eyes" before letting out a deafening roar. It then ran off into the darkness leaving the coach a wreck and the passengers and driver a petrified mess.

Such stories of beasts and Indian curses did not deter some investors from setting up a profitable enterprise in town. They purchased six square miles of land and formed the Bennington and Glastenbury Railroad, Mining, and Manufacturing Company. They then laid nine miles of steep railway along the mountain. The tracks were so steep that they ascended 250 feet per mile in some areas, making it the steepest traction railway ever built in the United States.

From 1873 to 1878, structures of all kinds went up. The town now had boarding houses for the workers who labored at cutting the lumber for the kilns. There was a blacksmith shop, a sawmill, a general store, a post office, and even a schoolhouse with four teachers. The curse seemed doomed itself. Then, the wood ran out. With no wood to cut, there was no more work. On June 3, 1890, the great mining company folded.

Some citizens remained, turning to fern picking and tourists for their means. They even built a hotel and used the railroad to transport the tourists in. Many times for free. It seems the curse would rise again as a great flood wiped out the tracks in 1898. By then people began to realize the Indian warnings were not just native superstition. Horrible reports of the ghastly creatures in the woods around the town were still circulating throughout the households. At times, the townsfolk could see eyes glowing in the night among the thicket as if waiting for an unsuspecting person to ramble into their realm. Now, only a handful of families remained.

In 1937, the town was officially unincorporated. By then only the Mattisons and Hazards, the two families who had been running the settlement since the beginning, made up the seven people residing within its boundaries. It would seem reasonable for them, being the original founders, to be the last to remain. In 1940, the Mattisons left the crumbling remains of Glastenbury. In 1950, the last inhabitant left as the elements and otherworldly entities won sovereignty over the domain. The woods remained ominous yet quiet, waiting for more victims to wander into their dark grasp. They did not wait for long.

The Long Trail, A part of the Appalachian Trail, runs through Glastenbury Mountain. On November 12, 1945, Middle Rivers, an experienced hiker of the Appalachian Trail, disappeared without a trace while on the familiar trail near Glastenbury Mountain. On December 1, 1946, Paula Weldon vanished from the trail. She was last seen hiking towards Glastenbury Mountain. Friends and authorities searched in vain for her. James Telford fell victim to the trail in 1949, and Francis Christman went missing in 1950. Other reports of vanishings and mysterious deaths have been reported. There are presumably ten disappearances that took place between 1945 and 1950.

Freida Langer was the only missing person to have actually been recovered from the path of evil. As she was hiking with a relative, she slipped and fell in a stream. She went back to the house to get dry clothes, but vanished into thin air somewhere along the way. Several months later, on May 12, 1951, her body was found in a spot that searchers had meticulously combed. The cause of her untimely death forever remains a mystery. Since then, many have shunned the path. Experts say there is a "hole" or opening to another realm that people unwittingly walk into, never to be seen again. Then there are the sightings of the creatures.

H.P. Lovecraft used the accounts of the ghost town to write "The Whisperer in Darkness." Lovecraft died on March 15, 1937, several years before the strange string of disappearances. This gives some sort of indication as to how long the paranormal activity had been surfacing in the haunted hamlet. To this very day, witnesses along the roads and paths that lace Glastenbury have ranted about the beasts that roam within the dark bowers of the Glastenbury forest and mountain. In 1996, an enormous creature, walking erect, stalked Donna Schneider while hiking through Glastenbury. Another man spent a night couching silently in one of the old cellar holes as a hideous creature rummaged around the site. Perhaps looking for its next prey. The sightings are continual as you read this writing.

The latest reports concern UFOs sighted over the mountain. Various sightings have sent researchers flocking to the old town in hopes of seeing something that will change their lives. The area is so ripe with strange unexplainable occurrences that it has been dubbed the "Paranormal Capital of Vermont." Somerset, next to Glastenbury, also shares a portion of the activity.

What did the Native Americans know that the settlers did not? Whatever it was, they learned soon enough. Now when one mentions Glastenbury to the locals, it can be assured that a shudder will run through most, and a look of dread will fill their eyes. Is the look for those who were there, or those who will be?

GLASTENBURY & GLASTENBURY MOUNTAIN

Glastenbury and Glastenbury Mountain (3748 feet) is in the Southwest part of Vermont next to Bennington. It is accessible by either the Appalachian Trail to the Long Trail between Woodford and Sunderland, or from a dirt road in Shaftsbury. Take Interstate I-91 into Brattleboro. Take Exit 2, Route 9 West towards Bennington.

HARTFORD

Haunted Railroad Bridge

Sometime between 2 and 3 in the morning on Saturday, September 5, 1887, Vermont's worst railroad disaster took place a few miles from White River Junction as the Vermont Central Railroad express train from Montreal jumped its tracks and plummeted onto the frozen White River below.

The train had been carrying many passengers from Boston. The engine was towing a baggage and express car, a mail car, two ordinary passenger cars, the sleeper car, St. Albans from Springfield and the Pullman sleeper, Pilgrim out of Boston. Many were on their way to see the circus in Montreal.

The 650-foot-long bridge spanned the White River at a height of 50 feet. At the time, subzero temperatures had formed a two-foot thick surface of ice on the river. As the train sped down the tracks, a broken rail about 200 feet from the viaduct caused the cars to slam into each other then pull apart breaking the coupling between the forward sleeper and the other cars. The engine, baggage, and smoking cars passed over the bridge safely but the other cars, striking the ties, came to the end of the bridge and completely wiped out the heavy beams resting on the abutment sending cars and bridge toppling onto the frozen river below.

The coaches and bridge then exploded into flames before the stunned onlookers' eyes. Forty people died in the wreck and another forty were badly injured or burned. The intense heat melted the ice in some places making rescue efforts all the more difficult. It is estimated that fifty to sixty people perished from the result of the wreck. According to legend, 13 year-old Joe McCabe was able to free himself from the burning, twisted debris, but watched helplessly as his father perished in the inferno.

The inefficient wooden bridge was later replaced with a steel overpass making it much more sturdy and safer. In time, people passing by began to notice a little boy near the river below. Many thought nothing of it but some noticed something was not quite right about the young man. His translucent appearance may have been enough to hint that he was not of this world, also the fact that he is seen hovering above the water that gives away his presence as being ethereal. Many witnesses have seen this apparition wandering the site below the bridge. Even paranormal investigators have had experiences with the ghost. There are a few more spirits that linger in the area as well. One is believed to be the conductor of the train who

was also one of the casualties on that fateful night. Many claim he walks the tracks making sure they are in perfect order as to avoid another deadly wreck. There are also claims of a ghostly locomotive silently rolling over the bridge with no cars attached to it.

Why the spirit of the young man lingers in the spot is a mystery. Some say it is the place his ghost returned to after he died due to the traumatic incident that he was part of, while others tend to think it is a residual entity moving about the scene of the wreck. He is seen

The present Woodstock Bridge in Hartford.
Photo courtesy of Victoria Julian.

hovering a few feet above the water, which would account for his being on the ice that was about that height at the time of the tragedy. Paranormal investigator and dowser, Stephen Marshall has actually felt the presence of spirit energy while dowsing at the scene. Either way, there are a few ghosts roaming about the White River. Take a trip to the bridge but beware of the phantom train that might silently steam by, or the countenance that might be spied hovering above the rocky stream.

THE WOODSTOCK BRIDGE

Spans the White River
and Route 14 in Hartford

Take I-91 to Exit 11 and
follow Route 14 to bridge.

INWOOD

Inwood Manor

Not all places become haunted after a tragedy. It is known that the site of a dreadful happening can scar the atmosphere causing either a residual or intelligent haunt. In the case of the residual haunt, the earth has taped the moment in time much like a CD or DVD recorder does. It then replays that moment at random, or perhaps when the atmosphere and environment is the same as when the moment was recorded. These are not actual haunts but rather a replay of a moment captured by the magnetic forces of the earth and surrounding accoutrements. The earth is magnetic, so why would it not be able to perform such a task? New England is full of underground streams and quartz, which together can act like a colossal battery storing energy and then dispersing it when the time is right. That time could be every eight hours or every eight years depending on the atmosphere and conditions that prevailed when the moment was recorded.

Intelligent haunts on the other hand are actually spirits or energy with the ability to interact and/or communicate with the living. They may not know they are dead or may have a message to convey. Perhaps there was some unfinished business or they just refuse to leave this plane of existence. As investigators, we are all still grasping at straws for many of the answers. Although we have some facts, there are still a lot of theories and unanswered questions to the phenomena we have encountered over the years. Every investigation is geared toward either finding rational answers to the occurrences or finding another piece to the great puzzle we call paranormal phenomena.

In the case of the Inwood Manor, the history behind the haunt is based on an account where a woman and her child drowned in the Connecticut River close by the edifice. No one ever raved about ghosts looming inside the manor so any history of a haunt would be scant, that is until the Inwood was renovated. This seemed to awaken the slumbering spirits who began to show themselves throughout the inn.

During the renovation of the thirty-two-room resort, owners Ron Kacsor and Peter Embaratto would witness who they felt may have been the woman who drowned in the nearby river. The woman suddenly appeared to them at the foot of the stairs. She was wearing a candy-striped dress and gave them a look of satisfaction that they figured might have been a nod of approval over the way they were remodeling the place. She then turned and floated up the stairs, vanishing into thin air at the top of the landing. They also noticed the countenance of a child following her and disappearing in the same manner. This child ghost would also be witnessed on the cellar stairs lending to the belief that they may be historical haunts that have taken up residence in the inn after their horrific tragedy. Historical haunts have the ability to move from one place to another much like that of a spirit seen in the kitchen and then perhaps in the yard or another room of an old colonial farmhouse.

The Inwood Manor is a beautiful place to get away and forget the strain of daily living. It has also become an eternal home for a few who have sought to escape the boundaries of the other side, that is, if there are any.

THE INWOOD MANOR

Inwood, VT

Twenty miles south of
St. Johnsbury on Highway 5.

JOHNSON

Johnson State College

Dibden Center

Johnson State College's humble beginnings date back to 1828, when it started out as an elementary school called Johnson Academy. In 1866, the state converted the school into a college intended solely for the training of teachers and renamed it Johnson Normal School. It became Johnson Teachers College in 1947 when the first four-year degree program was implemented. It was not until 1962 that the college got its present moniker and broadened its curriculum from just teaching to liberal arts. The college continues to expand with the changing needs for new and growing occupations. There are presently fourteen buildings on campus but one is of special interest to the students of the paranormal. That building is called the Dibden Center for the Arts. The building houses the music and theater faculty, studios, and practice rooms. It also houses classrooms, the Julian Scott Memorial Art Gallery, a 450-seat theater, and at least one ghost.

Arthur Dibden was president of Johnson State College from 1967 until his death in 1969. It was through his diligence that a new campus was built to accommodate the influx of students and educational expansion that had rendered the old buildings obsolete. Unfortunately, his demise came before the building of the new campus was completed. One of his favorite projects may have been the state-of-the-art theater that was later named in his honor. This could easily be why he has been given credit as being the ghost that haunts the edifice. It was erected on a precipice overlooking the town with the doors facing south. The finished construction was contrary to the plans that were originally to be implemented. Dibden wanted the doors to face north. This could be another reason why the strange goings on in the building can be attributed to him.

Each night after checking and confirming that the building was vacant of the living, the security crew would set the alarm and lock the front doors. Moments later the doors would fly open and the alarm would sing out in the night air. A search of the building always proved to be futile as there was no one inside that could have opened the doors and triggered the alarm. On many occasions, the staff would have to wait and close the doors several times before all would become calm and they could resume their duties elsewhere on campus.

Other doors open and close as if someone is moving about the building, and running water is often heard, yet no one has ever been able to find the source of the phantom flow. The toilet next to the Green Room in the basement is known to flush by itself every now and then. Plumbers have been called in numerous times to check out the problem yet they have always come out scratching their heads as to why it would be malfunctioning. It is related how Arthur Dibden, who was often on site, was known to use that toilet when the building was being constructed.

A giant spotlight once disappeared out from under everyone's noses only to reappear in the Green Room a few days later. The costume room is a place where people have seen apparitions and have felt presences. There is a lot of energy in the building. Some attribute it to the underground streams that are said to run under the center. It is known that such flowing water can create and store energy in a building. Coupled with quartz, you have a natural battery that can create a lot of energy. Another quaint fact is that a local show is taped in the building and one episode featured ghost and legend author Joseph Citro and Burlington author and haunted tour creator, Thea Lewis. They did not report any strange occurrences during their interviews. It could be that Mr. Dibden was too busy enjoying the show on his behalf.

Battery or bona fide boos; that is the question at Dibden Center.

JOHNSON COLLEGE

Johnson, VT

Take I-89 to Exit 10 Waterbury/ Stowe. Go North on Route 100 for 20 miles to Morrisville then bear west onto Route 15 for 8 miles into Johnson.

MANCHESTER

Rachel Burton

This next account deals with one the first known documented events of vampirism in Vermont. For the next 100 years, families across New England would desperately turn to folklore and through fear and superstition, dig up their beloved and perform exorcisms in hopes of saving the remaining family members from the wicked consequence of the vampire's wrath.

The year was 1793. America was a new nation with fresh opportunities, ideals, hopes, and fears. No one would have ever guessed one of those fears would come in the form of the undead. Born into the very young American culture was the notion that the dead were coming back from the grave to feed upon the living in the dark bowers of the witching hour. We must remember at this time that many beliefs, customs, and lifestyles were much different than what we know of in the present. Some were very strange, being born from fear of the unknown and superstition.

New England was prominent in the making of the nation, as well as the scene for this next gruesome true account of the fear that gripped the region in these supernatural times.

In 1789, Captain Isaac Burton married Rachel Harris. She was a strikingly beautiful woman with a charming personality. About a year into their nuptials, her beauty and grace began to quickly waste away. Her health was in a rapid decline as she mysteriously grew more and more ill. It was soon diagnosed that she had consumption, and within no time, it took her to the grave.

Within a short time following her interment, the captain married his second wife, Hulda Powell. She too was a handsome woman with a friendly nature. Soon, however, Hulda came down with the same dreaded infliction that took his first wife. Hulda's strength and vigor was waning fast and something had to be done without delay. The doctors had no cure for her and it was only a matter of time before she would follow the captain's first wife to the grave.

It was then that a strange belief took hold of the family and friends of Captain Burton. They concluded that the first wife was coming back from the grave and feeding on the lifeblood of Hulda. It was for the most part, the work of a vampire. Of course, they knew the body was not actually rising from her place of eternal repose and making its starlight morbid rounds. It was concluded that her spirit was leaving the tomb and feeding upon the living before returning to the grave each morning. Family and friends pleaded that Rachel's corpse must be disinterred and her vitals removed then burned. This ritual, already practiced in a few other places about New England, would surely exorcise the demon that wreaked havoc upon the Burton family. In February of 1793, they gathered at the gravesite of Rachel and began the task of ridding the family of their vampire.

Rachel had been buried for three years when the deed was carried out. It is reported that almost 1,000 people showed up for the gruesome exorcism. Her vitals were cut out and taken to the blacksmith forge of Jacob Mead. The decomposed liver, heart, and lungs were then reduced to ashes. Timothy Mead blessed the remains in an attempt to purge the demon that was sucking the life from Hulda. This form of medicine did not work as Hulda succumbed to the dreaded consumption on September 6, 1793.

Whether she was given the ashes to drink was not clear. In many cases of vampirism, the sick were given a concoction of medicine mixed with the ashes of the cremated organs. It would seem logical that the act of drinking that alone would be enough to finish off the sickly. The ways of the New England vampire were strange, but not nearly as strange as the cures carried out in hopes of eradicating their deadly "bite."

As of this writing, the burial place of the Burtons remains unclear. Isaac and his fourth wife were relocated from the Old Village Green to the Dellwood Cemetery when a courthouse was built on the site. Many unmarked graves are believed to still grace the green, including that of Rachel's and perhaps Hulda's. This is one perhaps you, the reader, might consider taking on yourself. You might want to consider going on a legend trip in order to find the exact whereabouts of the family.

The Equinox

The history of a number of Vermont's haunted hospitalities are as interesting, if not more illustrious, than their ghosts. In the case of the Equinox, they seem to go hand in hand. The story of the Equinox dates as far back as 1769. It originally was a tavern run by William Marsh. During the time of the revolutionary uprising and eventual war, the tavern was used for meetings on the imminent emancipation from England. It was at the Marsh Tavern that Ira Allen, Ethan's younger brother held a special meeting propos-

The charming and stylish Equinox Resort is reported to be home to the ghosts of Mary Todd Lincoln and her son as well as a former owner.
Photo courtesy of Victoria Julian.

ing the confiscation of properties owned by Tory citizens. A Tory at the time was a British sympathizer and therefore it was felt that these loyalists of the throne were a threat to the impending success of the war for independence. The sales of the property to supporters of liberty would help fund their recently formed regiment called the Green Mountain Boys.

The Legislature approved his plan on March 26, 1778, and the first property to be confiscated was ironically, the Marsh Tavern. William Marsh probably felt that the British were much too powerful and precise to let the colonies fall to a ragtag throng of revolutionaries so he sided with the Redcoats. Subsequently, the tavern was seized and Marsh migrated to Canada.

Thaddeus Munson purchased the property in 1780, where he later built a new inn next door. The inn changed hands three more times with Martin Vanderlip adding the fluted columns in 1839 that have since become a trademark of the historic inn.

The 200-room Equinox House opened in June 1853 under the ownership of Franklin Orvis, born in Manchester in 1824. He named the inn after the tallest mountain of the Taconic Mountain Range that towers behind the structure at 3,848 feet above sea level. The mountain itself got its moniker from Vermont Surveyor General, Colonel Partridge who reached the summit during the Autumnal Equinox in 1823. Various writings place Captain Alden Partridge, who became a captain in 1810 as Vermont's Surveyor General in 1822 so it may have been that particular Captain Partridge (as there were a few) who gave the mountain its name. *

Since then, there has been a long list of prominent people who have stayed at the Equinox. Among them are Presidents Ulysses S. Grant, Theodore Roosevelt, William Howard Taft, and Benjamin Harrison. In 1863 and 1864, President Abraham Lincoln's wife, Mary Todd Lincoln, and their two sons stayed at the inn. They truly enjoyed the hospitality and quaint Vermont lifestyle so much that they made reservations to spend the next summer there with the president as well.

A special suite was constructed for the accommodation of the first family. All precautions were made so that the president and his family would have a grand time during their stay in the Green Mountain state. The grand visit was not to be, for on April 14, 1865, the president was assassinated. The Lincoln family still remembered the wonders and tranquility of the area as Robert Todd Lincoln, son of Abraham and Mary, built his summer estate, Hildene just down the road from the Equinox.

Time went by and so did the heyday of the hotel. At one point, the rundown hotel became completely abandoned, and after the 1973 season, was boarded up. Francesco Galesi purchased the inn (he assumed the first mortgage in 1974, as the previous owner had fallen behind on mortgage payments) and performed extensive renovations. In 1985, the Equinox reopened as a year round resort. In the summer of 1995, the Equinox opened the Charles Orvis home to guests and in 2007 the thirteen-guest room 1811 House became another part of the resort's accommodations. This was the home of Abraham Lincoln's granddaughter, Mary Lincoln Isham, and her husband, Charles, from 1905 until her death in 1939.

Such a prominent and luxurious resort would not be complete without a few notable figures still roaming its corridors. The ghosts of Mary Todd Lincoln and her youngest son, Tad, are said to still frequent the hotel. Guests and staff have heard the sound of a child crying and a mother comforting it. Some have actually witnessed the ghostly pair in one of the guest rooms. A few of the witnesses recognized the apparition they had seen as Mary Todd Lincoln and her son based on a portrait. She seems to favor rooms 241 and 242, which were once combined into one suite to accommodate Mrs. Lincoln and her family.

The Lincolns are not the only spirits thought to still occupy the resort. Some believe that William Marsh has come back to his old inn. Perhaps he is attempting to reclaim the land that was taken from him when he sided with the British during the war. Could his ghost be responsible for the shades that were mysteriously cut up in room 440? Maybe he is the angry entity that ripped the pillows and blankets from the bed and tossed them all over the room shortly after the chambermaids had finished with the room. This would seem plausible, as the name of the room is called none other than the Green Mountain Suite.

Others believe that the spirit of George Orvis, son of Equinox founder Franklin Orvis is also still at the inn. George was the heir to the business his father had made so successful. In 1918, he strolled out to the pond to either go fishing or have a swim, no one knows for sure. Either way, he never returned. Could he be the cold breeze accompanied by footsteps in the hall in the dark hours of the night? People have heard the footsteps come up from behind and move aside thinking someone was in a bit of a hurry to get by. They would then hear the clatter pass them followed by a cold wind, but no physical entity to be seen. The staff at the inn have become so accustomed to the occurrence that they just move over and usher the unseen passerby on its way. Perhaps it might be either Mr. Orvis making ethereal rounds to see if the guests are all satisfied with their stay.

One night, the front desk received a call from Room 329. The guests sounded a little panic stricken so security and staff went up to check on their status. When they entered the suite, they were not prepared for what they were about to behold. The lamp shades were slowly turning on their spindles and the rocking chairs were swaying to and fro with no physical being to manipulate them. The guests were hastily and happily removed to an "unoccupied" room for the rest of the evening.

Guests also report being tapped by an unseen hand. They would turn to see who is beckoning their attention only to find that there is no one within arms reach of them. Members of the resort have concluded that it may be the son of Mary Todd Lincoln, as he loved playing tricks on people. Voices in empty rooms and other areas that are otherwise unoccupied help put a chill into the night air.

There are so many stories circulating in regard to the Equinox that it seems hard not to have a paranormal experience. But do not worry; there are 147 guest rooms and 3 suites in the main building alone (and 39 townhouses—the townhouses are a separate building, not in the main building), so if you do not wish to be visited by someone from the other side, there are plenty of other more "quiet" chambers.

The Equinox presently consists of the main resort building, The Charles Orvis Inn, Townhouses, Dormy House and The 1811 House. There are also restaurants at the inn that offer a toothsome cuisine that is out of this world. The Marsh Tavern offers a regional fare and a wonderful taproom. The Chop House is an upscale steak house. Fine food and spirits are plentiful at the Equinox Resort.

THE EQUINOX RESORT

Route 7A in
Manchester Village, VT 05254
1-800-362-4747
www.equinoxresort.com

Take I-91 to Exit 2 in Brattleboro. Take Route 30 North to Historic Route 7A. Turn left onto 7A and proceed for about 1 mile to the Equinox.

* (See the website for the Equinox Skyline Drive www.equinoxresort.com (Early History)

There are many legends concerning the name "Equinox." The one commonly accepted states that a certain Captain Partridge, at the time Director of the mellifluously entitled "American Literary Scientific and Military Academy," led a troop of cadets who marched from Norwich, Vermont, to what is now Manchester and ascended the mountain on September 19, 1823, for the purpose of making some barometric observations. Captain Partridge fixed the altitude of the mountain at 3,807 feet above sea level, which was surprisingly accurate for the times, the present altitude being 3,848 feet. The story goes that since the ascent of the mountain was made at approximately the time of the autumnal equinox, the mountain was thereafter refereed to as "Equinox Mountain."

MARLBORO

Marlboro College

Colleges and Universities seem to hold a lot of spirit. Not only in the dedication of the students to their alma mater, but also in the way that the other side seems to want to reside in these places of higher education. There are countless stories of ghosts and strange entities that run rampant among the many colleges and universities of our land. Some of these are no more than initiation pranks handed down from class to class. Their origins soon become lost to antiquity and a legend is born. Others, however, hold an indisputable validity to their paranormal happenings that even the most astute scholar cannot rebuke.

This would deem quite plausible, as many of these institutions are set among old farms or estates that have been provided for the purpose of bestowing an education to those who are ready to take on the world. Mansions, barns, and even blacksmith shops have been converted into classrooms and dormitories. It is little wonder that some of these edifices are still holding reminders of the past within their walls. To many, it is an education in history itself. To others, it is an education of terror. Marlboro College is no exception.

Marlboro is a typical quaint little Southern Vermont town with charming one-horse lanes and scenic landscapes that remain almost completely undaunted by time. Marlboro College, nestled away off the beaten path incorporates this laid-back essence that slows the hustle and bustle of life to a meandering pace where people can stop and take a breath or read a book while relaxing in the grass that once was home to cows and sheep.

The college was established in 1946 by Walter Hendricks for GI veterans of World War II. They settled on Potash Hill and used money received from the GI Bill to manage the school. Two farms also operated on the 360-acre site. Some of these buildings were later transformed to accommodate the growing student body. The old farmhouse is now an administrative building called "Mather" after

The Administrative Building at Marlboro College was once a farm house owned by the Mather family.

one of the previous owners. It is a typical eighteenth- and nineteenth-century structure one would expect to see in the rural areas of Vermont. There are a few others that remained when the farms transformed from the growing of food to the growing of minds. It is these buildings that can be seen to this day as one takes in the scenic wonder and tranquil setting of Marlboro College.

One such building is Dalrymple Hall. Dalrymple was a massive hay barn that was turned into classrooms by college handyman, Luke Dalrymple. In 1947, he, along with a number of students and faculty, renovated the barn to hold classrooms, faculty offices, and seminar rooms.

Another such building is the Outdoor Program Building near Dalrymple. This was a blacksmith shop converted to house the program and all its various equipment. Blacksmith shops were a very important staple on a farm. Mostly every tool was made of iron and when it broke, it needed

to be either repaired or replaced. There were no chain stores on every corner, so the farmer had to have a blacksmith close by to keep production of the farm going. Most New England farms had to be self-sufficient. Planting, tending, and harvesting of the crops had to be punctual, or the family would be very hungry that winter. Therefore, the farm equipment had to be always ready to take on the daily tasks necessary for survival in the rough New England climate.

These old buildings seem to still work in the eras that have past while mingling with the present. Nestled among the bucolic fields and woodland are a few ghosts. The most famous at Marlboro College is the ghost of Emily Mather. Like most traditions and stories handed down from generation to generation, the exact accounts are a bit hazy and in some cases have a few twists and turns to suit the storyteller's fancy, but for the most part, the end result is the same. Emily Mather haunts Marlboro College.

Darymple Hall, an old barn converted into classrooms is haunted by the spirit of Emily Mather.

Marlboro College graduate Caitlyn Paxson took a special interest in the ghostly legends of the college. She spent many hours collecting the story of Emily Mather. Her interviews and research on the ghost is recollected here in part with her permission for all to enjoy.

Emily was the daughter of one of the farmers who owned the vast tract of land and a good share of the little hamlet. Being of wealth, it was expected that she would marry within her stature, but Emily had other plans. She met a traveling salesman who she immediately fell for and they began courting. It was not long before the man asked for her hand in marriage and as expected, Emily's father stoutly refused to let his daughter marry a common traveler who sold wares. In those days, salesmen commonly traveled the countryside selling their goods from home to home and took to "tinkering" to supplement their income. This consisted of repairing pots and pans, sharpening utensils, and general fix-it jobs they may have learned along the way.

Legend states that the salesman was so distraught over Emily's father's refusal to give them permission to wed, that he was said to have wandered down to the brook by the pony farm where he threw himself in and drowned. Emily, upon hearing the news hanged herself in the barn. Since Emily had committed suicide, she could not be buried in the family burial ground, so they buried her west of the barn in an unmarked grave, which was later unearthed when Howland, was built. Howland was the first actual structure constructed for the college. Paxson wrote in her story on Emily Mather, "The western most rooms are said to be right over her grave."

Howland and Dalrymple

Research showed that there was no record of an Emily Mather, but in those days, people who committed suicide were often stricken from records pertaining to the

Howland Dormitory is also reported to be haunted by Emily Mather who was once buried where the building now sits.

family and cause of death. There is, however, lots of strange occurrences that have been blamed on Emily in both Howland and Dalrymple.

Students claim to have heard knocking under the floor as if someone was trying to get out. Some have seen a face in the window one moment and in an instant it is gone. Upon investigation, there would be no one around to have looked inside the western room. The doors open and close by themselves as if someone was entering or leaving and the most sizzling warm space heater is no match for the cold spots that permeate the room from time to time. A visitor to the dorms once saw a ghostly figure float across the second story balcony above the west room. A luminous green figure has been seen numerous times floating across the lawn in front of Howland. Others have seen manifestations and felt strange uncomfortable sensations while in the room.

Chris Lenois of Marlboro College helped to find out more accounts of ghostly activity on campus. Thanks to a written account by Jodi Clark and Caitlyn Paxson, along with Mary Coventry, called *Tales of Marlboro Ghosts* there are even more places than just Howland that have a few spirits still lingering as well.

Emily's spirit seems to roam freely about the campus much as she did when her mortal frame graced the grassy fields and buildings that was once her family's farm. There is a path that leads from Howland to the upper level of Dalrymple. It was there that a student got a lesson only Marlboro College's most famous resident ghost could teach him. As he neared the barn, he heard another set of footsteps behind him. He turned to see who it was but saw

A view of Darymple and Howland where the ghost of Emily Mather seems to move from one building to the other.

no one there to create the din. A bit perplexed, he continued on his short journey when the rustling of someone running and a hard shove sent him sprawling head over heels. He looked up at the top of the path and saw the pale image of a young girl in a white dress. The figure then vanished in front of the stunned student. People have also seen the spirit of a woman on the balcony at the library suggesting that Emily might be visiting that building as well. She is blamed for items that suddenly disappear within the library.

Every year, the college hosts a summer music festival where musicians gather to fill the fields and valleys with the sweet sound of their instruments. One of the festival hands, while passing by Dalrymple, happened to look up at the top windows and saw the figure of a girl holding a noose. The startled worker bolted into the building to the room where the girl was, but it had been long boarded up. He quickly summoned help in tearing the obstructions from the entrance. When they got the door open, the dusty, cobwebbed room was completely empty and long unoccupied, by the living anyway.

Whittemore Theatre

Two different ghosts are said to share the limelight in Whittemore Theatre. Audrey Gordon was not only the literature instructor at the college but she also directed plays there. While directing her shows, she would pace hither and thither across the back of the theatre. Individuals can feel a breeze in the back of the room as if someone is still pacing back and forth, wisping by them. Some have actually seen shadows out of the corner of their eye moving in the same direction as the wind. Stephen Greene is be-

Rice-Aron Library houses the spirit of a woman that students and faculty believe is also Emily Mather.

lieved to be the other spirit of the hall. The Greene Room within the edifice is named after him. Some of the stagehands and engineers hear strange noises in the catwalks or whispers, even voices while in the theatre at night.

Marlboro College seems to be full of spirits. Alumni and faculty will agree that there is never a dull moment at the sleepy little institution of higher learning.

MARLBORO COLLEGE

2582 South Road
Marlboro, VT 05344

Take Exit 2 off of Interstate I-91 in Brattleboro. Turn right onto Route 9 West for about ten miles. Watch for college signs. Turn left onto South Road. Stay on South Road for three miles until you come to the college.

Whittemore Theater has two spirits that share the limelight within the theater.

NEWPORT

Lake Memphremagog

General "Mad Anthony" Wayne's Ghost

Should you perchance be wandering along the shores of Lake Memphremagog and see an apparition walking with an eagle on each outstretched arm, do not be alarmed; it is only the ghost of Revolutionary War hero General Anthony Wayne who was born January 1, 1745, and died December 15, 1796, after a severe bout with gout.

Wayne began his military career at the onset of the Revolutionary War by becoming Colonel of the 4th Pennsylvania Regiment. His daring and bold personality attributed to his nickname, "Mad Anthony." In 1777, he was sent to Fort Ticonderoga to help Ethan Allen and the Green Mountain Boys. After a successful run of campaigns, he was promoted to Brigadier General.

There is a story of how he and a few scouts scaled a cliff in search of two bald eagles he wanted to train as pets. When he reached the nest, the eagles began to claw and bite him but he was undaunted in his efforts to retrieve the birds. He named them "North" and "West" with a surname of "Passage" due to the difficulty he faced in obtaining them.

Although he is buried in Radnor, Pennsylvania, his ghost seems to make a showing on the shores of the lake where his brilliant military career began to shine. Many have witnessed the ghost dressed in uniform wandering the shores with his trusty birds at bay. Some say he even floats across the water out of sight. His ghost is also seen in several other locales across the original thirteen colonies, but those are stories for another tome.

NORWICH

Norwich Inn

The allure of Vermont is exemplified by the Norwich Inn, from its Victorian charm to the ale pub on the premises that brews and serves its own hand crafted beers in small batches. Inns of yesteryear commonly brewed their own beers onsite. Many had special brewers to craft the exclusive libations that were served fresh from the kegs. Each tavern could boast their own private recipes for travelers to quaff and relish. Times have changed but not for the Norwich Inn.

The original inn was built as a mansion in 1797 and owned by Colonel Jasper Murdoch. Murdoch soon began welcoming stagecoach travelers while serving them fine home brews and fare of the day. President James Monroe dined at the inn on July 22, 1817, during his tour of New England, being the first U.S. President to ever be entertained at a Vermont inn. In 1889, the inn burned along with several other surrounding buildings. Dr. W.S. Bowles rebuilt the inn in 1890 from the original foun-

dation. It reopened in 1891, and was labeled by many to be the finest hotel in the region. The hotel has undergone many changes over the years but good old colonial tradition has never fizzled out. There are twenty-seven guest rooms located in the main inn, carriage house, and the vestry house, originally constructed in 1839 on the village green as a vestry house for the Congregational Church. The edifice also served as a meeting hall, schoolhouse, library in 1880, and post office from 1951 to 1961 before being moved to the present location behind the main building. Within the main building there is a fine dining room, and the Jasper Murdoch Ale Pub featuring the hand-crafted brews only available at the establishment. The Norwich Inn also boasts one of the largest wine cellars in Vermont. There are plenty of spirits to wet your whistle at the inn but there are also a few that might momentarily take the whistle out of you.

One is a woman in a long black dress seen gliding through the parlor en route to the library. She is believed to be the ghost of

The Norwich Inn has an illustrious history along with a ghost or two according to legend.
Photo courtesy of the Norwich Inn.

Mary "Ma" Walker. Charles and Mary once owned the inn and it is related that Ma Walker, in keeping with the reputation of the inn's penchant for serving fine libations, sold liquor out of the basement during prohibition. She is also seen on the upper floors as well. Other phenomena include faucets and lights suddenly turning on and off and rocking chairs swinging back and forth as if someone was enjoying their leisure time within them.

The spirits are not harmful in any way, just part of the magic that makes Vermont inns so special. In fact, the Norwich Inn is said to be the inspiration for the popular TV series *Newhart* that took place at a Vermont bed and breakfast. Owners Joe and Jill Lavin go out of their way to keep that magic alive for their guests. The ghosts are a big help as well.

THE NORWICH INN

325 Main Street
P.O. Box 908
Norwich, VT 05055
802-649-1143

Take Exit 13 off of I-91 towards US-5/Norwich. Turn left onto South Main Street/Trescott Road/VT 10A W. Inn is on Main Street.

PLAINFIELD

Goddard College

Music at the Manor. Sounds very enticing, does it not? The mind immediately conjures up an elegant soiree where the sound of a classical piano trickles through the room just under the din of conversations. Guests, dressed in formal attire relish in hors d'oeuvres and champagne while mingling and gabbing about the latest trends. This may have been somewhat of a typical scene when Willard S. Martin owned the home that he built back in 1908. The Georgian Revival-style structure served as the Martin's summer residence and although the grand balls may no longer be held, the sight of a piano still graces the hall and so does the sound of music. Occasionally, one phantom musician still basks in the revelry of eras gone by, as he is often seen cloaked in black and perched at the instrument.

Manor House

When Martin died in 1938, the property was sold to Goddard College. Goddard College began in 1863 as the Green Mountain Central Institute. It remained a seminary until 1937 when it became Goddard College. In 1938, the college moved to Plainfield. Since then, the facility has been a groundbreaking establishment for higher education known the world over. Almost as famous is the ghosts that reside within Martin Manor or the better known name of "Manor House."

A female ghost has long been a resident of the manor. No one is really sure who she is but they do know she is of the Victorian era by the way she is dressed. Doors slamming and strange footsteps are often heard throughout the Manor House when there is otherwise no one else in the building. A staff member once heard music coming from the house and made her way in to see who was at the piano. Upon entering the room, she noticed a man dressed in black seated at the instrument. The keys were moving but there were no fingers bouncing along them as the figure sat there motionless. Another incident involved a potential student who needed directions.

While passing the building she heard live piano music trickling from its interior. She made her way inside to seek help in finding her destination. There was a man at the piano that sat there and played yet heeded not her beckoning for his assistance. When she turned in disgust of his rudeness, the music stopped and a sinister laugh could be heard. She became frightened and headed towards the door. She turned quickly to see the man vanish before her eyes.

Garden House

The Garden House is another place of ghostly activity. It is in that area where the ghost of a woman is seen. Willard Martin was a descendent of Susannah Martin of Amesbury, Massachusetts, who was arrested on April 30, 1692 and executed for witchcraft on July 19 of that year in Salem. When he built the formal garden in 1920, he incorporated timbers from the old Ipswich Courthouse where the accused witches of the Salem witch hysteria, including Susannah, were held. When he had heard that the building was being demolished, he ventured to the region just north of the Witch City and acquired the timber for the building of his garden house. Perhaps it is the ghost of his ancestor or another of the accused witches that now roams the garden house. Maybe it is one of the members of the Martin family. Whoever it is, Goddard College has a lot of history and haunts to match. In a place where forward thinking is the norm, a remnant of the past kind of gives students a break from their obligations, at least for a while, anyway.

GODDARD COLLEGE

123 Pitkin Road
Plainfield, VT 05667

(Named after Goddard's first president)

Take Exit 8 off of Route I-89 onto Route 2 East. Before Plainfield take a left onto Route 214. College is first left.

PROCTORSVILLE

Golden Stage Inn

The Golden Stage Inn Bed and Breakfast offered travelers bed and board before Vermont became a state in 1791. Today, the four-season New England bed and breakfast reflects over 200 years of history in its eight guest rooms and one suite. There are four second-floor rooms named after members of the Skinner family who owned the inn for over 100 years beginning in the mid-1830s. The new wing has six additional rooms, all beautifully appointed. The solarium is one of three intimate dining rooms and was once the inn's greenhouse. Guests can cozy up to a crackling fire in the main parlor while exploring the inn's famous puzzle chest—a large antique box filled with unique challenges. The library has plenty of tomes to curl up with. On Halloween, the Golden Stage is transformed into a scary spectacle with spooky effects, creatures, and terrifying monsters. But it is the real ghosts that seem to get most of the attention, on Halloween or any other time of the year.

Sandra and Peter Gregg, innkeepers of the beautiful Cavendish bed and breakfast have become so familiar with their resident ghost that they have named him George. George is known to be a young and friendly specter dressed in a cloak and large brimmed hat. They do not know for sure the identity of the affable spirit but they do know he is harmless and seems to be attached to the house, so perhaps he was once an owner or past family member of the previous owners who have graced the inn's walls for over 200 years.

Our friends Robert Hughes and Victoria Julian paid a visit to the inn and talked to the innkeepers who are not afraid of their resident spirit. In fact, the ghost is quite welcome and has become an integral part of this lovely little four-season inn. They stated that they cohabituate with George and any other spirit they feel may also might reside at the inn. Here is the letter we received from Bob and Vickie while visiting the inn.

Bob and I met the inn-keepers, Peter and Sandy who, as they say, cohabituate with their friendly ghosts. They say that things get moved around from where they thought they left them, only to later find them in other locations. Their inn was a stagecoach stop and tavern. They showed us where the bar used to be back in 1788. Men stayed on the second floor and women on the third.

One night Sandy and her husband were sleeping in the innkeeper's quarters when Sandy saw a handsome man resembling Robert Redford, about 5'4"– 5'8" wearing a wide brimmed hat and a long black coat or cloak. At first, she thought it was a dream. When their daughter came home from college to visit, she stayed on the third floor. She thanked her mother for NOT telling her about the man that also staying at the inn. Sandy then realized that the man she saw was in fact a ghost and not a dream. They believe the man, whose identity is unknown, died on the way to save a girl.

Peter told us that the rooms in the newer part of the inn towards the rear of the building were the last to be rented. He stated that this is where there seems to be more activity. He thinks it's because that section is quieter. He said that a realtor took pictures of the inn but could not use them due to the fact that they had orbs in them."

As of this writing, the inn is up for sale. Perhaps, Peter and Sandy will change their minds and not want to leave their affable ghosts to someone else, or maybe the next owner will enjoy having them around as much as the present ones do.

THE GOLDEN STAGE INN

399 Depot Street, P.O. Box 218, Proctorsville, VT 05153

Take I-91 North to Vermont Exit 6, then VT Rte. 103 North through Chester (103N makes a right turn in Chester; don't miss it!). Proctorsville is approximately 8 miles from Chester. When you climb through the Proctorsville Gulf there is an additional climbing lane. At the end of the climbing lane is a sign that says "Golden Stage Inn 1/4 mile." Watch for the Proctorsville sign. Just after the sign turn right. The Golden Stage Inn driveway is 50 feet on the right.

A handsome ghost roams the halls of the Golden Stage Inn.
Photo courtesy of Victoria Julian.

READING

Bailey's Mills/ Spite Cemetery

As the shadow of Mt. Ascutney lingers over the picturesque town of Reading, a tale is told of one of the hamlet's most illustrious figures. In 1794, Levi Bailey (1766-1850) purchased a dam and mill in Reading. He became quite prosperous in his dealings and sought to expand his operation. His next-door neighbor, David Hapgood, owned a suitable parcel across the stream that Bailey adored and wanted to acquire. Unfortunately, Hapgood could not stand even the mention of Bailey's name and forthright refused to sell him any bit of his land at any price.

As the tolling of time went on, animosity grew deeper between the two. One day, Bailey shouted from his side of the river that the old man would soon have to pass on and when that day came, one way or another, the land would fall into his hands. Old man Hapgood, getting on in his years, knew this could well be the scenario, so he made provisions to assure that the land would be used otherwise.

David Hapgood died in 1829 and Levi Bailey was ready to claim his coveted piece of property he had so long waited patiently to obtain. Bailey, however, received quite a shock when he found out that the land he so desired had been donated to the town of Reading for use as a burial ground. To make matters more ironic for Levi, the first burial was that of David Hapgood and the tombstone was placed directly across from Bailey's front door. Every day, Levi Bailey would tend to his daily routine with the last vestige of Hapgood always just a glance away. It was a constant reminder of how, even in death, Hapgood was able to spite Bailey out of the land he so wanted to own in his lifetime. That is how the burial ground got its name. It is a moniker that has stood the true test of time, but not exclusively for David Hapgood.

Levi Bailey was not about to give up his conviction so easily. He straight out purchased a burial plot in the cemetery and when he died October 21, 1850 at the age of eighty-five, he was buried right near his nemesis in life. So you see, Bailey did acquire the land he so desired, although not as much, and not for life, but eternity instead. Perhaps this was his way of retaliating against Hapgood for his spiteful scheme in keeping Bailey from ever obtaining the acreage. Now they both share the same terra firma and can continue to spite each other enduringly. There is more to this story, however, that includes the building across the small lane from the parcel of eternal repose. It is known as Bailey's Mills Bed and Breakfast. It was once the home of Bailey himself.

Sometime between 1800 and 1850, the home sat among various businesses the prosperous entrepreneur built upon his property. Among them were a three-story woolen factory, a few smaller mills, and the ever-necessary blacksmith shop. Gristmills for grinding corn and grains into cornmeal and flour were a common sight along the banks of rivers and streams in early New England. Sawmills and tanneries were also commonplace along the edges of these coveted and busy waterways. The woolen mills were commonly three-story buildings with each level having a different responsibility in the process of making woolen communities. The first floor was set aside for the looms and spinning. The second floor was where the cotton and wool was cleaned and prepared for the looms, and the garret was usually designated for storage. Waterwheels ran these mills and used different styles to accommodate the needs of the industry. There were three types of wheel power in those days, undershot, breastshot, and overshot. Undershot wheels had the water run underneath them. This was not very efficient but very easy to construct and could be built alongside the river or very shallow stream. Small businesses could easily get away with the use of an undershot wheel. Overshot wheels were a bit more efficient as the water would fall into the buckets causing the weight to turn the wheel. This required dams and a series of sluiceways or raceways to bring the water up to a certain level in many cases and back to the watercourse. The breast shot wheel was actually the most efficient, as it would literally hit the wheel almost near the top with a predestined force, thus pushing the wheel around almost a full turn. This gave larger factories the power they needed to run the many looms and spindles they may have had. Care had to be taken to make sure the wheel did not run too fast or it would surely break the equipment inside the mill.

The blacksmith played a most important role in the early industrial complex, as they were the general "fix-it" men. Most of the tools and machinery were made of iron. It was essential to have the blacksmith on hand to repair or forge new implements as needed to keep the mills going. The blacksmiths had to forge their own tools in order to commence with their trade. That is what made them so precious and in demand. George Washington was reported to have

Bailey's Mills Bed and Breakfast is full of
history and perhaps a little mystery.
Photo courtesy of Victoria Julian.

two blacksmiths at Mount Vernon in Alexandria, Virginia. One was for the everyday needs of his estate and the other was for the constant demands of the people in the vicinity.

The Baileys had a general store where the employees would buy what they needed. This was common among mill villages and assured that the mill owners re-couped much of the wages they had paid out. The store is still in good repair and still in use as visi-tors soak in the rustic atmosphere of yesteryear and the wares that are within.

There are enough tales of Mr. Bailey to fill an afternoon in front of a crackling fire. One such tale concerns a young boy who was given a penny to splurge in Bailey's store. After much scrutiny over how he should spend his coin, he chose the largest fig in the box. Old man Bailey took the penny and examined the fig. He decided it was much too big a piece of pro-duce for just a meager cent and proceeded to take a bite out of the fig before handing the uneaten portion to the speechless child.

Along with the legend of the cemetery, there is a bit of "ghoulery and tomfoolery" associated with the bed and breakfast. Innkeeper Barbara Theader told me that, be-ing a place where engineers, scien-tists, and people of other pragmatic occupations meet, they do not generally believe in the paranor-mal, but there are a few stories. When she bought the house from her mother back in 1993, she was told that there might be a ghost in one of the bedrooms because a door would open and close on its own volition. One couple reported the incident to Barbara but she is not sure if anyone else has ever witnessed the moving door as those guests were the only she remem-bers who made mention of it.

A contractor came to the house to plan renovations. Barbara brought the group into the base-ment. As some of the workers sur-veyed the needed renovations, one of them asked her if there was any paranormal activity in the house. She stated that she was insensitive to such things but others might be more in tune. She then asked if he felt anything and he stated, "Oh yeah, there is a lot of activity here." She feels that if there is anything going on, it is completely harmless as no one has ever been bothered or hurt by anything.

One more little tidbit from Barbara comes in regard to the cemetery. Her husband, who is an engineer, caught a silvery glint out of the corner of his eye one night while quickly spying out among the burial ground. Barbara told me, "It seemed very shimmering and lively. He was intrigued, and crept cautiously out to the cemetery only to discover that exactly one memo-rial stone was polished enough to reflect the light of the moon. I think it really had him going for a while."

Bailey's Mills Bed and Break-fast is one of the more interest-ing places to stay, whether it is for legend or leisure, it is a rare gem. There are three charming rooms along with a garden room and library containing over 3,000 volumes for your perusal. There is a private pond where remnants of the mill can still be seen along the stream. There are also scenic back roads with cider farms and roving pastures. Who knows, perhaps old Mr. Bailey will want to give you a tour. If so, he might try to charge you a penny, or more.

BAILEY'S MILLS BED & BREAKFAST

1347 Bailey's Mills Road
Reading, VT 05062
1-800-639-3437
info@baileysmills.com

Take Interstate I-91 to Exit 8 for VT-131 towards VT-12 Ascutney/ US-5 Windsor. Take a sharp left onto VT-131. Take a right onto Amsden School Road. Bear right

The Inn at Rutland has a few friendly spirits.
Photo courtesy of Victoria Julian.

RUTLAND

The Inn at Rutland

An elegant Victorian mansion, The Inn at Rutland was built in 1889 by William F. Burditt. It is located within a few miles of Killington, Vermont. This Vermont Inn, voted Best Bed & Breakfast in the Greater Rutland area in 2000, 2001, 2002, 2003, 2004, 2005, 2006, and again in 2007, is a perfect place to stay for people skiing at Killington, hiking the Green Mountains of Vermont, or enjoying the fall foliage. Once inside the inn, you will feel as though you were back in the 1800s. The grand oak staircase, carved plaster relief ceilings and wainscoting, huge leaded glass windows, and fine period antiques all take you back in time to an era of romantic splendor. The Inn at Rutland has eight guest rooms on the second and third floors that are decorated in period fashion. The owners have collected all the Victorian furnishings personally. Each room has different trappings for a wonderful variety of choices to suit every taste. A few seem to have a ghost lingering as well.

The Burditt family had a caretaker named Henry. Henry was in charge of many of the various responsibilities that come with taking care of such an estate. One of his duties was to venture up to the attic where supplies were kept. He would sort out the week's provisional requirements then bring them down and prepare what was needed for the family. Henry had a fiancée who became very ill and died from her infliction before they could marry. This caused him to lapse into a deep depression. His melancholy nature worried the Burditt family who tried to help him get through his rough time.

One day Henry did not show up for his daily routine. The family grew a bit concerned. Several days later they had not heard from their trusted caretaker and became worried. In those days, people could not readily pick up a phone or email like they do today. Communication was slow and sometimes took days to convey correspondence of any kind.

Though worried over the disappearance of Henry, someone had to gather the family provisions from the attic. When a family member ascended into the garret, they were met with a most ghastly spectacle. There, hanging from the rafters was their beloved concierge, Henry, dead of apparent suicide. The distraught man had taken his own life.

Although Henry may no longer be in the flesh, he is ever-present in the inn. He makes himself known to guests and staff alike by opening and closing doors, turning lights on and off, throwing bath towels on the floor, messing up the freshly made beds, and other such little pranks. He is not a bad spirit by any means, just a bit mischievous.

Leslie and Steven Brenner now own the enchanting inn. I spoke with them in regard to their tenure at the inn and the ghost of Henry. They have owned the public house for over eight years and have not personally witnessed anything too peculiar in regard to Henry making his presence known to them. On one recent occasion, a guest who stopped in claimed to be sensitive to the dead and immediately sensed that there were spirits in the house. Another guest was speaking to a friend on the phone in one of the rooms and their friend, who was also sensitive, felt there were ghosts in the room with the guest.

Two people told Steven the building was once used as a boarding house. This is very common with old mansions. Many times they are purchased rather inexpensively due to neglect, and renovated enough to take on boarders. This enables the new owners to furnish

more restorations from the income generated by renting rooms. Many times, however, the theory is better than the result, and the home falls into decay.

Two different former tenants had seen the ghostly figure of a little girl on the third floor. She was witnessed standing in the hallway before vanishing in front of the startled lodgers. Who the little girl may be is anybody's guess. Perhaps she is one of the Burditt family that never left, or the daughter of a former renter. When a house goes through so many changes and people, it is extremely difficult to pinpoint the identity of former inhabitants, especially when they appear as wraiths many years later.

Steve told me that any presences that may reside there are by no means malicious according to guests and staff at the Inn at Rutland. He concluded, "They are very happy with how we furnished the rooms because the atmosphere is warm and welcoming."

Guests can enjoy a three-course breakfast complete with the finest selection of teas and Vermont coffees. Later, visitors to the inn can sit by the fire in the living room and enjoy a book or game. The ambiance is appealing, the area is picturesque, and the hosts are second to none. With such a wonderful surrounding why would they want to leave?

Rutland County is located centrally in the heart of the Green Mountains. Its beautiful scenic vistas and bucolic little village make it an irresistible four-season tourist stop.

The Inn at Rutland

70 Main Street/Route 7
Rutland, VT 05701
800-808-0575

From Boston Area: Take I-93 to just south of Concord, NH. Exit onto I-89 North and follow to US Route 4/Rutland (Exit 1 in Vermont). Follow US 4 West. Stay on 4 West until you intersect with Route 7. Make a right onto Route 7 North. The Inn is two blocks north on the right hand side.

From Hartford Area: Follow Interstate I-91 to North of Bellows Falls, VT. Take Exit 6/Rutland onto VT 103 to Route 7 North. Stay on 7 North for approximately seven miles until you go through Rutland. The Inn is two blocks north of the intersection where Routes 4 and 7 split.

SALISBURY

Shard Villa

It is hard to conceive that such an imposing structure as Shard Villa is actually a home for the elderly. Its ornate exterior is as mysterious looking and breathtaking as the interior, yet it does hold quarter as a domicile for elderly people to relish in its history, and as you guessed, ghosts.

The story begins in 1844 when descendents of Frances Mary Shard, who died in 1819, hired Columbus Smith as their attorney to fight a legal battle over money the throne of England was trying to take from them in regard to her estate. It took fourteen years, several trips to England, and a lot of paperwork but Smith got the job done and was rewarded handsomely for it. At one point, it is written that he argued the case for forty days, turning his hair and beard permanently and prematurely gray from the exasperating performance.

Smith returned to Vermont a wealthy man and made plans for a dream home. He found an idea and based his home on design #19 from an 1869 book called *National Architect* by George E. Woodward. Architect Warren Thayer drew up the plans and Joiners, George and Clinton Smith commenced building what would end up as a 2½-story cut stone French 2nd Empire 30-room mansion. The construction started in 1872 and by 1874, Shard Villa was ready for occupancy by the Smith family. Smith even hired a live-in muralist from Italy named Sylvio Pezzoli to paint the walls, floors, ceilings and other places throughout the house.

The Smiths lived pleasantly in their stately home for seven years until tragedy struck and Columbus's son, William, died at age 14 of a neurological infection. The loss of his son was a devastating blow to him and he began a rapid physical and mental deterioration.

Fourteen years later, his daughter, Mary Elizabeth, died and this loss reportedly broke what little spirit he had left. After Columbus died, the home was left to his wife who lived there until her death in 1919. The family is buried in a mausoleum on the property. In

SALISBURY

her will, Mrs. Smith requested that the home be used to house elderly citizens. An "L"-shaped addition was added in 1922 and has been home to many elderly citizens since. Some claim that the Smith family has never left the home.

Many have seen the ghost of Columbus wandering the dark halls and even meandering around in his former bedroom. At least they think it might be Columbus due to the gray hair the spirit sports when witnessed. He also is blamed for the doors that open and close with no human hand to perpetuate them. One staff member found a tub in an unused bathroom full of water. This would not seem so strange if it were not for the fact that the reason the bathroom was not being used was because the faucets for the sink and tub had been long rusted solid from time and neglect and could not be turned.

The sound of a piano playing and the breaking of glass is also heard quite often but when investigated, there are no signs of any glass anywhere that may have fallen. Another unnerving ethereal resonance that echoes through the villa is that of a baby crying. No one has ever been able to pinpoint where the reverberation comes from as it permeates the air with no particular area of source.

Who are the ghosts of Shard Villa? Are they remnants of the past replaying over and over? Are they intelligent spirits looking to communicate with the living? Could Columbus Smith be making an occasional rendezvous through his old manor to make sure the terms of his wife's will is being carried out to his liking? No one is sure as yet, but perhaps someone will someday be able to better communicate and acquire an answer from the spirits that seem to happily inhabit Shard Villa.

SHARD VILLA

1177 Shard Villa Road
West Salisbury, VT 05769

Take Route 7/Ethan Allen Highway to Farmingdale Road then take a left onto Shard Villa Road.

STOWE

Green Mountain Inn

The Green Mountain State has no shortage of extraordinary characters that are laced throughout its history. From the Green Mountain Boys to Allen Morse's Frozen Vermonters and everything in between, Vermont is without a doubt a state where New England legends abound. One such legend is the story of Boots Berry. Now the story goes way back a bit but you might just get a chance to meet old Mr. Berry if you happen to pass by the Green Mountain Inn and decide to stay a spell in room 302. You see, that is where this legend began.

The inn itself has a captivating history. Peter Lovejoy originally built the present 100-room inn in 1833 as a private residence. He then decided to trade the property in 1850 to a man named Stillman Churchill for a 350-acre farm. Churchill obviously had plans for the estate and began adding to the building. Before long, two wings and a dance hall were implemented into the main structure. He then

A green vortex is seen in front of the Green Mountain Inn. Could this be the spirit of Boots Berry waiting to hitch a team of horses to the next stage?
Photo courtesy of Victoria Julian.

added a double porch in the front and opened it as the Mansfield House. Financial difficulties forced a foreclosure on the property and the lodge was soon transferred to W.P. Bailey who named it the Brick Hotel.

It was Mark C. Lovejoy who named the hotel the Green Mountain Inn when he acquired it in 1893. The Mount Mansfield Electric Railroad came to town and a depot building was erected next to the inn in 1897. The inn would change hands several more times with renovations and restorations making it modern but with old-fashioned embellishments throughout. Even the depot building next door was renovated into four luxury suites. One of the latest additions being the Mansfield House featuring twenty-two rooms including twelve luxury suites and the other being new townhouses with full kitchens, living rooms, and other conveniences. There is also a library, health club, two restaurants, game room, and a year round outdoor heated swimming pool. The inn is a mixture of modern amenities and historic antique Vermont flavor that is evident throughout the rooms. There is also the resident ghost.

The ghost is said to be that of Boots Berry, a local icon in Stowe who later became a tap dancer. Boots was born in room 302 in 1840. He was the son of the inn's horseman and chambermaid. During that time, the third floor was reserved for use as servant's quarters. Young Mr. Berry grew up at the inn and later took over his father's position as horseman for the inn. His duties were to provide the fresh horses that the stagecoach needed to continue on its next leg of what were sometimes long journeys through the Green Mountain State. Inns usually kept teams of horses in their stables that were part of a certain stage line, replacing the tired steeds for a fresh team that could continue the journey to whatever destinations the coaches were headed for.

One morning, he was fulfilling his duties as usual when the stagecoach team got spooked and began bolting down Main Street with a coach full of frightened travelers. Boots, in a valiant and brave moment, managed to get a hold of the stage, stop the horses and save the passengers. He was promptly awarded a hero's medal for his courageous deed. News of his bravery spread like wildfire and before long, there was not a tavern in the region that would dare charge him for a drink. As wonderful as this may sound, it was also his downfall. Boots's penchant for the free libations and neglecting his obligations as horseman led to his dismissal at the inn. He then migrated down to New Orleans where he was jailed. It was there that he learned to tap dance.

Boots eventually returned to Stowe in 1902, broke and hungry. It was about the same time he rolled into town that a terrible snowstorm followed in his wake. A little girl somehow became stranded on the roof of the inn as the snow piled up making it impossible for anyone to reach her. Boots, having grown up at the inn and exploring every nook and cranny thoroughly during his childhood days, remembered a secret passage that led to the spot where the girl was trapped. Mr. Berry speedily made his way onto the roof and lowered the girl safely to the ground. Unfortunately, no sooner had the girl reached the ground safely below, Boots slipped on the icy roof and fell to his death. The part of the roof he was on before he fell was over room 302, the same room he was born in. He was once again a hero, but now in death.

Our friends, Robert Hughes and Victoria Julian opted to stay at the Green Mountain Inn during their trek across Vermont. Armed with ghost hunting equipment, they investigated the inn from top to bottom, but did not get any strange activity within its walls. There was however a strange anomaly that turned up when Vickie took a picture of the inn from the outside. In the photo there is a green light or vortex moving upward or towards the ground. Sources told her that was the spot where Boots Berry fell from the roof to the ground below. What could it be? Who knows? But it is rather strange to have such an anomaly in the spot where legend was born. Perhaps the ghost was letting them know he is still on duty at the inn. Although after all, many of the staff and guests already know that.

When the winter's bite seizes the region and the snows begin to fall, people in the inn begin to hear a shuffle on the roof over room 302. They know it is the spirit of Boots Berry tap dancing above the room where he was born and in the end, became once again, a hero.

THE GREEN MOUNTAIN INN

18 Main Street
Stowe, VT 05672
1-800-253-7302
info@gminn.com

Take Route I-89 to Exit 10 and follow Route 100 for 10 miles. The inn is located on Main Street (Route 100) at the intersection of Route 108.

Emily's Bridge

When John N. Smith designed the fifty-foot covered bridge that stretches over Gold Brook, he boasted that its unique features would make it eternal upon the land. He never would have expected it to harbor one more eternal feature not included in the plans, the vengeful spirit of a young woman named Emily.

The bridge was erected in 1844. Some claim it to be the oldest covered bridge in America. Whether it is or not is a topic of debate, but the very old haunt that the span possesses is indisputable. The story takes place around 1849, a few years after the bridge was built. A young woman named Emily Smith chose to accept the proposal of marriage from a certain gentleman. By some accounts, the apple of Emily's eye was a local lad of ne'r do well fame while others say he was a new figure in the sleepy little hamlet. Either way, the parents of the bride-to-be were outraged. They did not take a liking to her suitor at all and made it very clear that she would not marry the man so long as she remained within the domicile. Emily was stubborn and steadfast in her plans to wed the man who wooed her. The couple decided to elope and begin a new life somewhere else, away from her demanding parents. They made secret plans to meet at the Gold Brook Bridge in the cloak of darkness and steal away into the night.

There are conflicting accounts as to what happened next. The first account that I had heard many years ago was that, in her haste to be punctual for their rendezvous, she somehow overturned her carriage at the bridge and was either killed in the fall or drowned in the stream.

Another account is told of how she arrived at the bridge only to find a note from her love stating that he could not marry her as he was promised to someone else and had already left town. The thought of being spurned by her lover left her distraught and irrational. As she sat and pondered, time gave rise to the sun. By sunrise, Emily had hanged herself from one of the rafters on the bridge.

Still, one more story is circulated that blends elements of the two previous narratives in regard to the fact that he actually refused her at the bridge and rode off. In an attempt to win him back she raced her carriage over the bridge but failed to negotiate a turn and met her fate when the carriage flipped over.

What became of her future husband is not known. Either way, she has never left that spot. In fact, she makes a point to let it be known that she is ever-present and quite angry in the place she spent her last living moments. Scores of individuals have felt the presence of Emily. Many have taken photographs of the bridge and discovered genuine orbs or even misty figures looming within their pictures.

She sometimes appears as a bright light hovering just above the ground in wait for the next unsuspecting passer-by. The life-sized spectral luminosity has spooked more than anyone cares to count over the centuries. Her vengeance comes in the form of strange sensations to downright painful afflictions. Some have felt a heavy sorrow, while others reported severe unexplained pains in the neck that befall them instantly while at Emily's Bridge. The pains would vanish without explanation as they reared from the vicinity of the foreboding viaduct. There are tales of horses being scratched or clawed while attempting to cross the bridge. The visible marks on the animals were a sure sign that Emily was not happy with their being at her bridge.

Even people and their automobiles have felt the wrath of Emily's unearthly talons. One group of legend trippers parked at the bridge in hopes of confronting the ghost of Emily. They got more than they bargained for as a white misty figure began to hover about them. In a fit of panic, they hurdled themselves into the automobile as the figure took on the shape of a woman with the devil in her eyes. She seized the door handle and began to shake the car violently. They then heard a horrendous clawing sound that resembled knife blades scraping against steel. The frightened group sped off in haste. They later inspected the vehicle and found claw marks on one of the doors.

This is not the only relation of this nature concerning Emily. There are many narratives written in various tomes that describe the same actions of the ghost of Gold Brook Bridge. Whether these accounts are true or not I cannot say. There are witnesses

The famous Gold Brook Bridge or "Emily's Bridge" is favorite destination for paranormal researchers and legend tripper alike.
Photo courtesy of Victoria Julian.

who have seen the specter calling for help, or witnessed a white form in the middle of the road as they pass over the bridge. Some stop, most know better.

In 1969, major plans were drawn up by a developer to build a housing project near the span of spectral occurrence. They were quite shocked to find that no one would ever occupy a dwelling within that close proximity of Emily's eternal home. The idea was scrapped and Emily was given credit for the termination of the considerable construction venture.

Paranormal researchers have flocked to the bridge in hopes of communicating with Emily. A lot of them have gotten photographs of orbs or strange mists. A few have gotten a more detailed human form glowing by the haunted overpass. Sensitives have felt her presence most fervidly and become utterly apprehensive by the energy she is said to exude. There have been a lot of personal paranormal experiences, but it was our friends and fellow paranormal researchers, Robert Hughes and Victoria Julian, who got what appears to be a rare EVP of Emily at the bridge. Emily is not known for verbalizing but the uncanny wailing on the recorder shows that she may have finally had something to say and Bob and Vickie were there to record it.

It was their second vigil at the bridge during the late hours of the evening when the gibbous moon shone down upon the span. Bob began to beckon Emily to speak and speak she did, not once, but twice, twenty-six seconds into the record-ing and thirty-eight seconds into the session. Of course they did not hear it at the time and are trained to state if any strange but explainable noise is heard that may later be construed as paranormal. The flow of the river provided a perfect white noise background that many investigators say is essential for EVP work. The voice can be heard above the sound of the watercourse as if it was very close to Bob. Maybe it was.

The first EVP sounds like a hello or moan. It is barely audible but the second comes after Bob asks, "Emily, are you here?" A voice answers with what sounds like, "Who likes to know?" They asked several more questions pertaining to why she is still at the bridge, but did not get any more answers. Perhaps she did not want to talk to them or maybe that was all she had to say. Maybe she wants the haunting to remain a mystery so the populace can keep returning for her rancorous amusement. It is one case that has made many mull over and some tremble with fear. Will Emily ever rest in peace? The answer might lie in the future, or maybe even in eternity for if the bridge was to last that long, then Emily will be there for a long, long time.

EMILY'S BRIDGE

Stowe, VT

(Officially known as the Gold Brook Bridge)

Take Interstate I-84 to Highway 100 into Stowe. Gold Brook Road is a few miles out of town. The bridge is on Gold Brook Road.

WATERBURY

The Old Stagecoach Inn

The accolades of the Old Stagecoach Inn speak for themselves about the experience you will have staying there. There are eight individually decorated rooms, three suites, relaxing parlor, library bar, full country breakfast, and more. Vermont hospitality is like no other, as you will soon read, by both the residents you can see and those you can't.

The history of the inn is full of colorful characters that helped shape the very enchantment that emanates throughout. It is a few of these characters that still keep residence at the Old Stagecoach Inn to this day; namely, Margaret Annette Spencer, or "Nettie" as she was called.

The history and stories that follow are told in greater detail on the Old Stagecoach Inn website. Special thanks to John Barwick for sharing them with us; this is a prime example of a good old-fashioned Vermont ghost story.

The inn was built in 1826 by Dan Carpenter, a former judge, along with his brother. However, according to recently found documents, the inn was constructed by a Mr. Allen with Horace and Henry Atkins as carpenters and joiners. The original owner is named as Mr. Parmalee. It was used as a stagecoach stop, meeting house, and secret gathering place for the local Freemasons.

In 1848, the railroads were laid through town and this action began a trend of tourism for nearby Stowe. Many of these travelers spent a night in Waterbury while on their way to the big resorts that Stowe had to offer. The Old Stagecoach Inn was there to accommodate them. By 1898, the trolleys were clanging down Main Street replacing the outmoded stagecoach altogether. The modern age had come, but it was not until the 1930s that automobiles would succeed in becoming the main staple of transportation along the streets of Waterbury. Families were now trekking by motorcar through Waterbury to Stowe and the inn was still there to give them a good night's rest.

A kind elderly lady in a long black dress has been witnessed wandering the building and welcoming guests to the Old Stagecoach Inn in the middle of the night.
Photo courtesy of Victoria Julian.

The Henry family bought the estate from the Carpenters and kept it as an inn in one way or another. The Henry family was prominent in town and one of their eight children, Margaret Annette Henry who was born in 1848, was a bit prominent in personality. High spirited and bold, she smoked cigarettes when it was taboo for women to do so, she even went one step further by chewing tobacco when she chose. She married Albert H. Spencer, wealthy socialite who was the owner of a number of factories and pieces of real estate in the area. The couple owned several homes and apartments around the world including France and England. The farm in Waterbury was renovated from an inn and residence to a lavish Victorian style manor with no expense spared.

Albert died in London in 1907, and Mrs. Spencer removed back to Waterbury to make the manor she had known in her younger years her main abode. Rumors circulated about the aging woman from how she poisoned her husband to running a moonshine operation in the cellar of the home. In her later years, she went deaf and needed a horn to hear but nonetheless remained quite active in business affairs. She died in 1947 at the age of 98.

The property was then sold to C.B. Norton who operated a private business from the home while still renting rooms for extra income. When Mr. Norton died in 1972, the building had begun to fall into disrepair and was now being used for low-income boarding. Mrs. Norton sold off the rear property and some furniture to pay for its upkeep as best she could but by the time she passed away, the edifice was unfortunately in shambles. That is when Kim and James Marcotte purchased the structure in 1985 and began renovations with the help of the historical society. The inn opened two years later and was once again a familiar favorite on Main Street. Five years later the inn was once again vacant for a year and a half until John Barwick and John Jr. reopened its doors for business. They even bought back the portion of back yard that had been previously sold by Mrs. Norton years before.

Today, the inn is a beautiful attraction and place to stay. It is typical of the scenic Vermont that everyone sees and imagines while visiting the Green Mountain State. Hospitality reigns at the inn by everyone, including, according to this next account, Mrs. Spencer. Mr. Barwick is a bit of a skeptic when it comes to the paranormal but he still cannot figure this experience out. He offered this story:

It was a busy summer weekend at the inn and all the guests that night had been present for Sunday morning breakfast. The dining room was still mostly full. Mr. Barwick was helping the waitress, by keeping the coffee urn and orange juice pitcher full, and by removing dishes. All rooms were booked, but the reservation for room three had been unexpectedly cancelled the previous evening. Mr. Barwick had taken the cancellation himself, and no one knew about it but he.

As he was standing at the dining room entrance two people came down for breakfast. They were unfamiliar to him. He had registered all the other guests and chatted with many of them, so he had a pretty good idea who was staying there. He thought perhaps it was a couple come in from off the street looking for breakfast, which occasionally happens. But it was odd that they had come down the stairs instead of through the side door. To make sure, he asked if they were guests of the inn.

"Yes," they replied. "We're all in Room Three."

"How many of you are there?" Mr. Barwick asked.

"Three," they answered.

"Three," said Mr. Barwick, "That room accommodates only two. Where did you all sleep?"

"Oh, we managed," they replied. "We couldn't find a place to stay. This was the only one."

Still puzzled, Mr. Barwick asked, "Well, what time did you come in?"

"Oh," they said, "it was around two-thirty this morning."

"Well, who let you in?" asked Mr. Barwick.

"Why, it was a lady, an older lady. Very nice."

More puzzled than ever, he now asked, "What did she look like?" thinking it might have been one of the other guests who had been unaccountably awake at that hour.

"Gray hair, kind of in a bun, and wearing a long dress," they replied.

That didn't match any of the other guests. But even if it had been another guest, it would have been extremely unusual for them to have unlocked the door and allowed three people to come in for the night. And how could they have known that the room was available?

After the newcomers had been seated and their orders taken, Mr. Barwick queried the other guests as they left the dining room to see if anyone had any knowledge of the incident. No, no one did. He thought for a long time about this. There was probably a logical explanation, but he couldn't think of it then, and can't think of one now.

And there it stands, a small mystery among many. Maybe not enough to certify the inn is haunted, but very odd, nevertheless.

Our friends Bob Hughes and Vickie Julian visited the inn during a week-long excursion through Vermont in search of the perfect destination for their wedding. They found the inn and innkeepers to be most charming and welcoming. Mr. Barwick narrated this next account to the couple as they sat and chatted about the inn.

A man and wife had arrived mid-morning, claiming they had stayed at the Stagecoach Inn about twenty- to twenty-five years ago. They had stayed in Room Two where they had seen the ghost of a woman standing at the edge of their bed. They described her as an elderly lady in a long black dress wearing her hair in a bun.

One morning the staff was cleaning the rooms when one of them came down in a flutter from Room Two. It seems that someone had lain on the bed despite the room being empty for some time. The woman, Margie, went back upstairs but came flying down to the first floor again in a huff ranting that now there was another strange occurrence. Jack went upstairs to see what was causing such a commotion. In a matter of a few moments, the bed had been stripped down to the mattress and all the sheets and pillowcases had been neatly folded.

Other guests have claimed to have witnessed the lady in a long black dress with her hair in a bun wandering about the house. Perhaps it is Mrs. Spencer still making sure her business is tended to or she might be relishing in the way the inn is cared for with such a meticulous flare for the Vermont charm. If so she may never want to leave.

THE OLD STAGECOACH INN

18 Main Street
Waterbury, VT 05676
1-800-262-2206

Take Exit 10 off I-89 and turn left at bottom of ramp onto Route 100 South. Travel 300 yards to intersection then take left into center of town. The inn is on the right.

WILMINGTON

Averill Stand

In 1751, John Averill (Averell) paddled up the Connecticut River, then called the Great River, with his family by canoe. He settled in a region that had been labeled as No.1 under the Massachusetts Charter. The area was new to the English who had only recently driven the French from the land. That is probably why they gave it such a low numerical moniker. At that time, there were but two houses on 10 Rods Highway. The first was at the foot of Willard's Hill built in 1739 by Richard Ellis and his son, and the other was at the top of the hill at the southern end of the street. Four men, one woman, and two children occupied it when the Averill family moved in. John and his son, John Jr., both fought in the Revolutionary War. It was around this time that his family began a migration from Massachusetts to Vermont. Before that, they were among the early settlers of the new world, having placed their roots around 1640 in Ipswich and Topsfield.

It took over 100 years for them to leave Massachusetts. Even the witchcraft trials of 1692 could not displace them from their settling ground, despite the fact that Sarah Averill Wilds and her cousin were both wrongly accused of making a pact with the devil. Sarah was arrested on April 21, 1692, and was hanged on July 19 of that same year. The name of the cousin is unclear although there were two other innocent people from Topsfield who went to the gallows as well, Mary Easty, arrested April 22 and executed September 22, and Elizabeth How who was arrested on May 28 and hanged on July 19.

In 1786, James Averill from Palmer, Massachusetts, purchased the first parcels of land in Wilmington. It was on the steadily traveled Molly Stark Trail in 1787 that Averill Stand was built. The public house was the main stage stop between Bennington and Brattleboro. It was a stagecoach stand, tavern, and inn, hence the name Averill Stand. In 1797, he deeded the land to his son, Benjamin. The Averill family remained owners of the property, living at Averill Stand,

Avery Cemetery
Photo courtesy of Victoria Julian.

until 1917. The family cemetery adjacent to the pasture of the farm/inn is full of the Averill clan where a lot of family history can be learned while scanning the stones. There are some, though, who occasionally return to the house they once knew in life to remind the living that they are still watching over their legacy.

Lavina Field Averill is reported to have died in the house while giving birth to her child. Her spirit is known to steal items and personal belongings. These objects are almost always found on the kitchen counter at a later date. A visitor to the old stage stop once witnessed the wraith of a woman dressed in very old-style clothing in the dining room. The woman faded away into thin air.

Between 10:30 and 11:40pm, the owner's dog would frequently run to the back door, barking and howling as a strange figure would cross the back yard. The ghostly form would make its way through the yard to the old carriage lane before disappearing. The doorbell has rung on snowy nights, yet when the door was answered, there was no one at the threshold and not a single footprint in the snow leading up to the house.

It is also claimed that the spirit of Mrs. Brown who was married to lumber baron Martin Brown haunts the house. Her home, the White House of Wilmington is very close to Averill Stand. It is recollected in some writings that she lived at Averill Stand in the early twentieth century. Perhaps she migrates back and forth to alleviate the boredom of haunting just one house. Her ghost is also reported to haunt her own home, the White House, as you will soon find out.

Present innkeepers of the stand, Jim and Bob have many stories to tell to those who stop by for an evening at one of the more interesting stops along Route 9.

Their hospitality is second to none and the rooms are wonderfully decorated. The stay includes a continental breakfast and free soft drinks as well as all the time you want to spend with the farm critters. Don't forget to make some time for the ghosts, as they are a part of Averill Stand's history that cannot be missed.

AVERILL STAND

236 Route 9
East Wilmington, VT 05363
802-464-9951

Take Route I-91 to Exit 2, Route 9. Follow Route 9 West into Wilmington.

The White House

Beautiful homes and the New England landscape seem to go hand in hand. They grace each other's company with a complimenting balance of nature and planned architecture. There is one such place that stands sentry on the top of a knoll along Route 9 in Wilmington. Its majestic appearance makes for quite an awe-inspiring sight. The fact that it is a bed and breakfast makes it more

The elegant White House in Wilmington where Clara Brown may still reside long after her tenure on earth.

enticing. Throw in a ghost and you have a place that is a must stay in this quaint little hamlet.

Arlene and I visited the White House on a beautiful May morning. New owners Philip Filleul and Stacey Tabor greeted us with a friendly smile and a lot of stories to tell. Much of the conversation was on how the newly acquired lavish mansion-turned bed and breakfast was receiving a prim and proper preparation for their future guests. Exquisite appointments and fine-tuning were the work of the day for the two new owners and their staff. The couple had recently arrived from England where they decided to make a go of it at a country inn. What better place than in Vermont, and what better place than in a haunted hotel. Philip has no problem with the White House having a harmless ghost or two. He grew up in a haunted house and was very excited about the fact that there

might be a spirit in the building, specifically Room 9.

They had just closed on the building a few days previous but were well aware all the stories of its history and haunts. At the time, they had not seen or heard anything in the mansion. The spacious manor's original moniker was the House at Beaver Brook Farm and was a summer home built in 1915 for lumber baron Martin Brown, his wife, Clara, and their three children, Ina M., Roy S., and Emma A. Both levels were designed with hand-crafted French doors, fourteen fireplaces, and stunning porches offering fresh air and panoramic views of the Green Mountains. It also boasted an indoor bowling alley and nine-hole golf course. One item of particular interest that Martin and Clara had installed for unknown reasons was a secret stairway behind a downstairs cabinet that led to an upstairs

Room 9 was Clara's room. She still lets occasional guests know.

closet. Perhaps it was put in to add a little playful mystery to the home, perhaps more. The real reason may be lost to antiquity but guests can still slink into the passageway and emerge in the upstairs closet as mysteriously as they vanished downstairs.

Mrs. Brown loved her summer retreat and made all attempts to decorate each of the twenty-nine rooms with the perfect touches that made the mansion feel like a cozy and quaint little home. She was especially proud of showing off the décor as they entertained guests who would relish in the extravagant wallpaper printed in France (some remains to this day in the front hall), mahogany walls, and fine rugs. After Martin Brown's death in 1962, the property was sold and the Martin's summer home became an elegant and romantic country getaway. The White House, as it became to be known,

had opened its doors to the outside world in 1965, but there existed, within its interior, another world that the White House catered to as well: the spirit world.

Bob Grinold owned the inn before Philip and Stacey took the keys to the establishment. Having purchased the mansion in 1978, he and Adam Grinold had many stories to tell of the manor that might just suggest the Martin family is still lurking within its walls. Strange noises are common in old houses but some of the clamor within the White House defies rational explanation. Strange creaks and groans permeate the building at all hours and the doors open and close by themselves, or so it seems.

One chambermaid complained that the closet doors would slam shut when she entered certain rooms. The presence responsible usually waited until she was close to the entryway of the closet before

slamming the door in her face. At first Bob thought it was the work of a ghostly imagination more than an actual presence, but slowly things began to convince him that maybe there was someone else in the house, someone left over from another era.

A guest staying in Clara's old room came down for breakfast one morning with a very peculiar tale to relate. Sometime in the darkest hours of the night she was interrupted from her slumber only to find an old woman reclining in the rocking chair next to the bed. The creaking of the chair may have roused her from her sleep but she was now awake and someone else was in the room with her. The old woman had her hair tied up in a bun with a shawl draped across her shoulders. At first the guest thought it was a dream but the old woman spoke. "One Mrs. Brown in this room is quite enough." The elderly matron's words echoed in the room as she vanished, leaving the empty rocker swinging to and fro as the creaking trailed off into the night air. The nature of her words may have been confusing at first but it was later discerned that the guest's last name was Brown.

Most of the activity centers around Room 9 where a lot of Mrs. Brown's original possessions are kept. One of the staff witnessed the doors on either side of the fireplace in that room open then close, one after another. The horror-struck girl exited the guest chamber in record time. Her last name was also Brown.

Another couple stayed at the inn while their children slept in the room next to them. In the middle of the night the children rushed into the parents room ranting of an old woman that materialized before them out of thin air. When the startled parents entered the kid's room, they found the same rocker, now located in that room swinging back and forth with no one in it. Ethereal voices call out to chambermaids but when the staff attempts to locate the source of the utterances, they find the area void of the living.

There is an inexplicable cold spot that Bob and others have experienced in the kitchen near the old butler's pantry. He has held a lit cigarette there to see where the draft might be but the smoke just wisps straight up as the air is quite calm around the room. The events that have occurred at the White House have left both staff and guests scratching their heads, but one thing is sure, if Clara Brown is still roaming about the estate, she certainly enjoys the way old and new owners have made it a beautiful place to stay. It is timeless in its ambience and permanent residents.

Follow directions to Averill Stand and go just past the stand to the White House.

WOODSTOCK

Woodstock's First Vampire Case

Woodstock seems to have a very diverse history when it comes to the paranormal. Recollections of ghosts, strange monoliths, and even vampires are part of the illustrious past of this Vermont community. It appears that around the time of the Mercy Brown case in Exeter, Rhode Island, there was much ado concerning the New England vampire. Articles appeared in almost every known publication from small town "rags" to major scientific journals. The vampire frenzy in New England had certainly raised eyebrows worldwide. Scores of cases went unreported while others such as this next account was penned much later as one man recollected his life in prose. This particular case took place in 1817, but was not acknowledged until the latter half of the nineteenth century.

The case of Frederick Ransom was written by his brother, Daniel, in his unpublished manuscript,

Memoirs of Daniel Ransom. Although the script was written many years after the incident, when Daniel was in his eighties, it still brings home the dilemma the New England people faced in regard to the evil disease, consumption. It is a classic example of how families turned to folklore and superstition in their desperate attempt to stop the dreaded infliction that was taking their loved ones to the grave.

Twenty-year-old Dartmouth College student, Frederick Ransom died of consumption in 1817. Fear that other family members would be taken to the grave by the young man caused the father to have his son exhumed and his heart cut out and burned. Daniel was only three years old at the time but the eerie incident stayed as vivid in his memory as the day he bore witness to the bizarre procedure.

It appears that consumption, the early name for tuberculosis, was hereditary in the Ransom family. Even young Daniel was told that he would never see old age as the malady would surely claim his mortal frame in due time. It was also related to his kith and kin that if the heart of one of the family members who died from consumption was removed and burned, then the rest would be spared the horrible suffering and eventual ultimate death from it. Their father, being perhaps a bit desperate and superstitious, ordered his son's body to be exhumed and his heart to be burned at Captain Pearson's blacksmith forge. The cure however, failed to work as Mrs. Ransom died in 1821, followed by his daughter in 1828, and two sons in 1830 and 1832.

The account was published in the Vermont Standard in the 1890s. The manuscript written by Daniel Ransom still exists in the Williams Public Library on Woodstock Green. Mr. Ransom's superstition was not a rogue example of turning to folklore for a cure in this case, as many held the same beliefs along with other "cures" for the frightful disease that wasted away whole families. When medical science could not provide answers or relief, many turned to folklore and superstition to fill the void and afford hope that such remedial efforts might put an end to the infirmity that was ravaging through New England households.

WOODSTOCK

Woodstock is located east of Rutland on Route 4.

From Boston, take Interstate I-93 North to Interstate I-89 North into Vermont. In Vermont, take Exit 1. At bottom of ramp turn left on Route 4 West. Travel 10 miles to the center of Woodstock.

From Connecticut and points south, take Interstate I-91 to Exit 9 (Hartland/Windsor) in Vermont. Follow the signs for Woodstock and Route 12 North. Take Route 12 approximately 8 miles. Take a left onto Route 4 West (Routes 4 and 12 are now merged), through Taftsville. Stay on Route 4 West for 3 miles to the center of Woodstock.

From the west, get on Route 4 East and follow into the center of Woodstock.

The Mysterious Corwin Case

In 1830, another vampire exorcism was said to have taken place in Woodstock concerning a family named Corwin. Much like the other tales of New England's undead, a family member, this time named Corwin, had succumbed to consumption. Another member of the family, a brother, soon exhibited signs of the same disease. A certain Dr. Joseph Gallup was credited with telling the family that as long as there remained blood of the sick brother in the heart of the deceased, the terror would continue until the second Corwin was taken to the grave. This implied the work of a vampire. There was only one solution, cut out the heart of the evil demon sucking the life from the family members and end the trepidation once and for all.

The deceased was exhumed from Cushing Cemetery in Woodstock as a crowd assembled on the green. It is written that most of the town showed up to witness the exorcism. A fire was cast on the green and the heart of the exhumed brother was cut out and burned to ashes. The ashes were then put into a pot to be buried in a hole that was dug in the center of the village green. Some of the ashes were saved for use as medicine for the ailing Corwin.

The pot was then put into the fifteen foot deep hole and covered with a seven-ton slab of granite.

The townspeople then sealed the hole in hopes of vanquishing the evil that had befallen the Corwin family. After the pot had been interred, the superstitious throng sprinkled the freshly turned earth with bull's blood. The dying brother was made to drink the mixture of ashes and bull's blood along with some medicine in order to cure his illness. Whether the cure worked is a mystery, but so is the whereabouts of the Corwin family as well as the slab and pot.

Records show no existence of a Corwin family interred in the Cushing Cemetery. Even the green has been excavated in search of the seven-ton slab of granite and pot of ashes. Nothing of the sort has ever been found. Could the facts have been diluted over time? Perhaps the names were misspelled or changed by accident. Maybe it was another town. Whatever the answer may be remains a missing piece of the puzzle in the search for the mysterious New England vampire.

See above for directions to Woodstock and village green.

Stones to the Stars

Almost everyone has heard of the great Stonehenge in England. There are many more of these megalithic structures gracing the European landscape. These prehistoric configurations chart out the paths of the sun, moon, and stars. They coincide with seasons as well as the major pagan holidays.

Many of their origins remain a mystery to modern man. But, even more of a mystery is how such astronomical stone calendars of European origin end up scattered about the New England countryside?

Although Christopher Columbus is credited with the discovery of America, many of his peers traveled the eastern seaboard of the land during the same era, charting out the territory. It appears that some civilizations were here long before Columbus and his colleagues landed on the sands of North America. Giovanni de Verranzano mapped out the Rhode Island coastline and in the process made note of a stone tower sitting in an advantageous site upon a hill of what is now Newport. He also wrote that the local Indians were of a whiter skin and more civilized than other Indians he had met. Roger Williams, credited founder of Rhode Island, made the same discovery. He also found that the Narragansett Indian language contained many Norse words. This led to the conclusion by him and later scholars that the Narragansett Indians were inbred with the Norsemen of Greenland. Verranzano also made mention of their taller stature than he or the other natives of the land. When he published his map of the area in 1524, he named Newport, "Norman Villa." Incidentally, the Newport Tower is reported to possess an uncanny resemblance to Norse villas built on the coast of France. Even he, however, was a late pioneer of the new world. Archeological finds in New England have uncovered countless relics left behind by the Vikings, Phoenicians, and Iberian-Celtic people who ventured here from the Icelandic territories to trade or find refuge and peace in the new world as far back as 2000 BC.

Many of these cultures were sun worshippers and erected their temples to the skies in order to track time and seasons with amazing accuracy. It is these remnants that stand to this day in the middle of forests and fields, lacing hillsides far above the valleys that baffle even the most astute scientists. One such site is called "Calendar One."

Archeo-astronomer Byron Dix came across a bowl about twenty acres across in 1974 while looking for a stone chamber he had heard about in South Royalston, Vermont, not far from the White River Junction. In the center of the bowl was the chamber, but around the bowl sat more than he could have imagined. He noticed a stone row running north and south with mounds on each end. The mounds had grooves cut in them. He also made note of three slabs of quartz about three feet high and five feet long. Two of them had window-like grids carved in them. These were easily recognized as the ancient Iberian-Celtic symbol of sun worship.

He returned in 1975 to take photos and chart out the area. His research found that the Spring Equinox fell in perfect line with the stone row. Later he would observe the Summer Solstice rise at the northeast peak and set at the northwest notch in the hills above.

It seemed that nature had created the foundation for a megalithic calendar that some race added upon. The Vernal and Autumn Equinoxes lined up with peaks of the hills as well. Two standing stones on the east ridge marked the Summer and Winter Solstices.

After further investigations, more standing stones were found notched into bedrock and buried over time with about three feet of soil. These were used to mark out the eight point Pagan calendar. This calendar marked out Spring, Summer, Winter, Fall, Beltane (Mayday), Imbolc (February mid-winter), Lammas (midsummer), and Samhain (November 1st, the Pagan new year).

From an astronomical stand-point, the alignments suggest that Calendar One is a little over a thousand years old. Other stone chambers were discovered along the hillsides surrounding Calendar One. Much of this site mirrors those found in Europe dating as far back as 4000 BC. The bowl, though not an effective location for a pre-historic celestial calendar by choice, had many natural markers of notches and peaks suggesting that the builders of the sky chart and its surrounding stone chambers were there for quite some time.

Some twenty miles south of Calendar One, on a dirt road off of Route 106 in South Woodstock, Vermont, sits what is labeled as Calendar Two. Unlike Calendar One, this site has been meticulously laid out on a hill, not in a bowl, using very few natural notches and peaks as sight lines. The road leading to the site is scenic and small, full of farms and very steep at some points. It is not the type of route a person would expect to travel while witnessing an ancient mystery. We could not take pictures of the area but the description of Calendar Two is clearly charted from the trek my wife and I most diligently made there and the great information available from the New England Antiquities Research Association.

A viewing platform of flagstone with another stone propped on top sets the stage for witnessing the changing of the seasons. Its corners are in perfect line with the Equinox sunrise and sunset. A perfect European Pythagorean triangle of stone abuts the platform. The walls measure 136 feet in length, or, 50 megalithic yards. The apex of the triangle points perfectly to 0 degrees north. From the platform, one can look across the end of each wall to a triangular cornerstone and witness the Summer Solstice sunrise come in full view over the hills directly over the point of the cornerstone. The layout of this triangle is no accident. There are other such triangles found about New England. Another Summer Solstice observation point sits a few hundred feet from the platform. This site is marked with ancient Ogham inscription. Ogham is an ancient Celtic script found in many places throughout New England. The script chiseled into the rocks and monoliths at Calendar Two contains only consonants. It wasn't until after the birth of Christ did vowels slowly make their way into the archaic alphabet. The point stone at the apex of the triangular wall also contains Ogham inscriptions.

Viewing straight across the platform at another boulder inscribed with Ogham symbols, one can witness the Winter Solstice sunrise. A 19- x 10-foot stone chamber on the property faces the same Solstice sunrise. Its dimensions also coincide precisely with the 18.61-year lunar cycle. Nearby is a pre-historic quarry where evidence of stone chisels had been used to break rock away from the ledges for use in the Calendar Two site. Byron Dix also found many stones around the area inscribed with symbols used by ancient Western Mediterranean civilizations.

These findings of the quarry, the 18.61-year lunar cycle alignment, the scribed stones, and the other factors conclude that the area was obviously populated by an ancient civilization for quite some time.

For more information or to arrange a visit to either site, you can contact the New England Antiquities Research Association at www.neara.org/into.htm

Ghost
HUNTING
GUIDE

A BASIC REFERENCE FOR PARANORMAL INVESTIGATIONS

By Paranormal United Research Society (P.U.R.S.)

Good Luck and Happy Haunts,
Paranormal United Research Society

www.**nepurs**.com

Ghost hunting is nothing new. Plato (427 – 347 B.C.) wrote of ghosts prowling the sepulchers of his homeland and Pliny the Younger (A.D. 62? – c.113) wrote of a villa in Athens that no one would rent because it was haunted. Shakespeare (April 23,? 1564 – April 23, 1616) wrote of ghosts and apparitions in his plays.

Lets fast forward a bit. In 1673, John Briggs beheld the ghost of his sister, Rebecca Cornell of Portsmouth who had burned to death. He then went to the Magistrate in Newport, Rhode Island, claiming that his sister, who had supposedly died by "unhappie accident," was actually murdered. They exhumed the body and found wounds in her abdomen made by some sharp object. Her son was arrested and convicted of murder, as he was the last to be with her in the room while company awaited his return just beyond the threshold of her room. It is said to be the first time in American history where a spirit condemned someone for murder.

Thomas Edison (1847-1931) was an avid ghost hunter. He believed that we were made of "life-units" and they could be traced after death. He set out to build a communicator for this purpose. He patented hundreds of inventions but died before he could perfect his ghost-communicating machine. He considered his works failures because none of them succeeded in reaching the other side. Among these "failures" were the electric light and the phonograph.

Many ghost hunters would follow, Harry Price, Elliot O'Donnell, and Harry Houdini, to name a few. In their times they did not have any sophisticated equipment like we do today. They relied on their feelings, intuition, and homework for the astounding results they achieved in finding the prowlers of the past. A lot of investigators today do not use all the bells and whistles that are on the market. Many rely on a camera, recorder, and their keen intuition and experience to find and log evidence of the paranormal. They believe that if you cannot show a picture or play back a voice from beyond, what good is trying to convince someone a ghost caused your EMF meter's movement or thermometer's temperature fluctuation? Armed with a camera, tape recorder, and a few other simple gadgets, you too can find the source of haunts as well as any machines, if not better. Remember, the best tool you have is your own intuition and instinct.

Appearance or experience of a deceased or disembodied life force, spirit, or "soul." Apparitions are the visual appearance of any spirit phenomena including ghosts. We are all electrical in nature. Energy is not created or destroyed, only transferred. When a living creature dies, its energy may either stay intact or disperse. Sometimes a person may not know they are dead. We all have an aura that is nothing more than our energy or electrical field emanating from us. Strong auras could stay intact while weaker ones disperse. Although we have many facts in regard to the paranormal, much of it still remains theories in regard to what really causes paranormal phenomena. Until we can go to the other side, hang out for a few months and come back, we are basically looking at the whole spectrum of what causes paranormal phenomena from our side of the veil. Other objects such as ghost trains may just be residual or place memories. This will be explained below.

ENERGY: Items moving, cold spots, wind, or physical contact.

These are forms of communication from the other side that take on a more physical nature. A spirit may move items or touch someone in attempt to communicate. Cold spots and wind are also forms of paranormal phenomena. If an energy force is moving, it will cause a breeze. If it is trying to manifest or communicate, it needs energy from another source. That is why the temperature might drop during an occurrence. The entity is drawing energy out of the atmosphere in its attempt to communicate. We have also seen batteries in the equipment drain almost instantly when this happens.

MANIFESTATION: Full figure, hazy form, orbs (not necessarily a haunting), or oblong light shapes.

Full figures are rare but most unsettling. They may be residual in nature or a manifestation trying to impart something upon the living at that time. Hazy forms are probably unsuccessful attempts at full manifestations. Perhaps there was not enough energy to draw from at that moment. No one is really sure. That is why this field is so interesting and wide open. Every new finding, no matter how small, is important. Orbs are balls of energy. Since energy is everywhere, it does not constitute a haunting, although, where ghosts are reported, there are orbs. There are theories as to why, but we are still grasping at straws. They could be attempts at manifestation or residual balls of energy after a phenomenon. They could also be there because a place is loaded with roaming energies for one reason or another.

VOICES: Whispers, audible, or inaudible words.

Vocal attempts at communication are nothing new. Capturing them on a recorder is. Disembodied voices are a form of spirit communication that we can now capture on tape or digital recorders. They seem to be the most common of communication from the other side as far as "physical" evidence is concerned. We have heard twenty times more EVP (Electronic Voice Phenomena) recordings than we have seen photos of actual apparitions in any form.

Types of Haunting.

HISTORICAL: A type of haunting that pertains to ghosts found in historic areas or homes.

They mostly appear in solid form, many times unaware of your presence. They can appear in more than one place throughout the site. They are not usually aware of your presence as they go about what was once their daily routine in life.

ATMOSPHERIC OR RESIDUAL: An imprint or recorded moment of the past that replays at random.

The earth is magnetic and can record much like our various electronic recorders, CD, DVD, VCR, digital, and other such modern devices. When conditions are right, it replays that moment just like one would replay a CD or DVD. This has also been called Stone Tape Theory or place memories. Some claim it is light particles that remain suspended in the air until an outside force stimulates them. These haunts are very common and are often confused with other types of haunts. Residuals can often be historic as well. They need not be born of some tragedy, although, a scarring of the earth's energy field from such a shocking moment can cause the magnetic field to trap the event. They replay at random. When the conditions are right (maybe the same as when the moment was "taped") the event is replayed. It could be anything from a person walking or standing in a spot to a whole battle being reenacted. These are not dead people trying to communicate as much as a replay of a past moment in time.

CRISIS HAUNTING: Before or after death or tragedy.

Many people speak of a loved one coming to them before or after that person has met with disaster or their passing. The loved one is trying to communicate before passing over to the other side. If you think about it, you are tied to this person through family DNA, or a bond of love, or both. It would seem easy for their energy to link with yours for that moment.

HAUNTED OBJECTS: Attached energy, either negative or positive.

Objects being made of molecules, of course, can store energy as well. When something is hot or cold, it has stored the energy that it was exposed to. Simple physics prevail here. But why, or how, does it store energy of a past owner? That we can theorize in many ways. Perhaps the owner loved the object and imparted a bit of their energy or aura into it or, maybe it was part of a moment that created a residual haunting and was later passed on away from the place of the residual haunt.

OBJECT APPARITIONS: Buildings, cars, etc.

Many speak of the factory in Uxbridge, Massachusetts, that burned down but would appear at times as if it was still thriving with life and production. These types of phenomena are an enigma for sure. How can an inanimate object appear or disappear? Perhaps it has something to do with a mixture of energy, molecule makeup, and the atmosphere where it is. Again we do not know for sure. It could be just a plain old residual haunting.

POLTERGEISTS: Caused by the living.

Science has found that poltergeists are created by a living being. Mostly children who reach puberty and are feeling the transition from childhood to adult. They become "agents" of energy that collects in them unwittingly and then shoots out creating havoc. Yes, this energy can be of spirit nature. It has been found that evil spirits, good spirits, and what some call demons have collected in a single area where this type of occurrence is taking place. Poltergeist activity can also be born from stress, frail mental state, anxiety, and suppressed anger or frustration.

Places to go Ghost Hunting

CEMETERIES

These are good places to start. Some think that spirits are drawn to their physical bodies that are buried there. Others say it is because they knew they would be there later, as the rest of their family is interred there. No one knows for sure why cemeteries are haunted. They just are. Always respect the rules of the cemetery and touch nothing.

SCHOOLS

Every college seems to have a "spirit" or two roaming its campus.

HOSPITALS

This goes without explanation. Many patients who have died in the hospitals may still linger.

BATTLEFIELDS

Such powerful energy, as the terrible experiences during fierce and bloody battles, will definitely leave a place with psychic scarring. Thus they are ripe with the ghostly reenactments of those brutal moments in history, or those who fell defending their beliefs.

HOTELS

These can be home to many spirits, former owners, or guests, either due to tragedy or happiness, and former staff. There are many cases where hotels are still staffed by long-dead maids or butlers.

RESTAURANTS

Many restaurants were also old taverns and inns once. They could harbor many entities of the past. In old New England it was mandated that a tavern should be placed every five miles for travelers. Very few people had horses, and even fewer had carriages of any kind. Most of them walked, and the journeys through the region were even tougher in the long New England winters. Taverns were places where news was posted, mail delivered, meetings were held, and social events took place. Usually, they were across from the local meetinghouse. After the service, it was common for congregation members to rush over to the tavern to bask in the warmth of the fire and partake in some drams of rum. This much activity could easily lead to later activity long after the people have passed on.

HISTORIC LOCATIONS

Some spirits linger in these due to the love they had for them in life. Some might have been born of tragedy, while others could be a passing moment in the history of these sites. A lot of these places are owned by historical societies that have acquired furniture from all over. The pieces themselves may hold some energy from the past as well.

Equipment

TAROT CARDS

We have discovered that the use of tarot cards during our investigations have produced astounding results in regard to finding answers to questions or discovering information that would not have been known to us before. The cards not only act as a medium but also help us with the energy at the site in question.

The cards are an ancient form of divination that everyone, including spirit energy, is familiar with. Arlene is a gifted reader who credits her success to the surrounding energy. She has an uncanny ability to let it flow through her. She does not claim to be psychic, as the cards and the subject are the catalysts. She is just the reader and interpreter. The cards seem to open a channel of communication that gives us more information to use when trying to discover exact identities and purposes behind a paranormal occurrence.

The results have yielded many answers in the form of EVPs and other discoveries that when researched, proved to be historically factual.

During one reading at the Ramtail Factory in Foster, Rhode Island, Arlene drew a card that prompted her to ask the question, "Who is the woman in charge of the finances?" When we listened to the recorder, a faint voice answered "Orra Potter." Upon researching the history of the mill, it was discovered that Olney Potter died suddenly in 1831, leaving his wife Orra with the majority of the shares in the business.

Various forms of EMF meters all work with the same principle. A compass can be used when the EMF levels in an area are too high or when batteries "mysteriously" drain instantly during an investigation. They are called the "poor man's EMF" but have proven quite effective and reliable when the regular meters fail.

EMF DETECTOR
(Electromagnetic Field)

This device measures the electric and magnetic fields that move in right angles to each other at the speed of light.

Paranormal occurrences disrupt these fields and cause the meter to jump or spike. When using one, follow the guidelines below for best results.

- Take a test reading of the area and log it, then continue moving about the room comparing your original data.

- Look for electrical devices, test them and log how far their field radiates.

- Spikes in the meter might indicate paranormal nature.

- Keep meter two feet from you or anyone else and away from your wristwatch or other electrical equipment you may be carrying.

Equipment

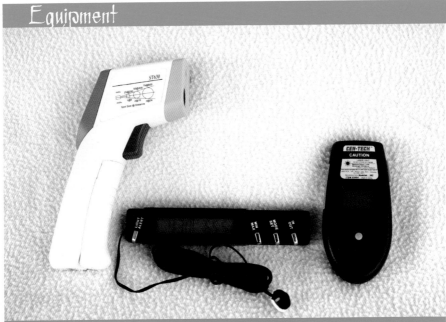

Thermal infrared thermometers and a digital thermometer are good for taking air and surface temps at sites. Regular mercury thermometers are just as effective. They can rationally explain cold spots or lock onto moving paranormal entities. Sudden drops in temperature can also be signs of paranormal activity.

THERMAL SCANNER
This measures temperatures of surfaces at a distance.

They can pinpoint cold spots from a distance. They are also good for finding moving orbs or vortexes. These are not completely necessary but can be handy. Electronic stores have inexpensive versions for about $20 to $40.

- Take general readings of area and log.
- Temperature changes could be drafts, bad insulation, cracks in building, removed from heat source, or paranormal.
- Rapid temperature drops could be energy contact. Moving drops could be orbs or other paranormal phenomena.
- Work in conjunction with EMF detector and regular air temperature thermometer for more conclusive results.

Two-way radios are very important when multiple teams are investigating a site. Communication between teams is crucial in helping validate or debunk possible paranormal occurrences.

TWO-WAY RADIOS
Communication from room to room is helpful.

- You do not need expensive units, as you will not be traveling miles from each other.

BATTERIES
A must have.

- It is known that energy trying to manifest can drain batteries instantly.
- Have plenty of fresh batteries on hand.

FIRST AID KIT
We all go "bump" in the night at one time or another.

FLASHLIGHT
A must have.

- Take plenty of batteries. Shaker flashlights are also great. If something is going to drain their power, you can just shake it and continue.
- Headworn lights are better because they free your hands.
- Opt for lights with colored lens covers if possible. These can be bought at any department or army/navy store. Also try colored mini LED lights.

Equipment

Various recorders include digital and tape recorders. Either one is just as good as the other. The best EVP we ever got was from the cassette tape recorder we bought for $1 at a yard sale. The "Shack Hack" box is a special recorder that picks up frequencies in real time. Thomas Edison spent many years trying to perfect this device, which he is credited for originally inventing. Frank Sumption finished where Edison left off. If there is a spirit voice present, it will be heard at that moment.

RECORDER
One of the basic and valuable tools of the trade.

You do not need an expensive recorder. In fact, the lesser expensive recorders get the same amazing results when looking for EVPs (Electronic Voice Phenomena) as any expensive unit. Electronic Voice Phenomena is the art of capturing spirit or ghost voices on tape or digital recorder. One of the best EVPs we ever captured was recorded on a recorder we bought at a yard sale for $1. The ghosts are not going to say, "Don't speak to that person; they have a cheap recorder. Lets wait for someone with a better recorder." If they have something to say, the recorder will capture it.

- Always have extra tape and batteries.

- Tape immediately upon entering a site while setting up. We have discovered that when we enter a haunted place, the spirit energy becomes curious or peaks. If you record immediately, you might have their attention. After a while, they lose interest and go away. We have seen and heard many cases where evidence was lost because nothing was running while setting up for the investigation and something paranormal occurred. We walk into the place in question with a recorder and camcorder already running from the start in order to capture any evidence of the paranormal. Again, the ghosts or spirits are not going to say, "No, wait until they set up to move that glass." When they want to communicate, it is your responsibility to be ready for them.

- Ask if the spirits mind you recording them. Ask if there is someone who would like to speak to you. If you know a name ask if they are present.

- Be polite. It has been proven the nicer you are, the better chance of getting a positive EVP.

- Why you will not hear a reply. Since paranormal activity is electrical in nature, you will not hear their voice reply. When we talk, our voices are acoustical in nature. A recorder's microphone basically uses a transducer that changes the acoustic air pressure into electrical current that can be processed and replayed. A spirit bypasses the acoustical part and goes right to the electrical process. That is why your ears will not pick up an answer. If you do hear a voice, you are very lucky as that type of communication requires a lot of energy and is rare.

- How long to record: Ask a question then let the recorder run for about fifteen seconds. You should tape for about five minutes maximum. Listen to your results. (See below for more information.)

- Note that the regular tapes are known to capture voices due to the ferrous oxide and chromium dioxide on the tapes. Digital does not use tape so how do they capture ghost voices? It could be due to the quartz that is used in modern equipment to enhance battery life. Perhaps that aids in capturing these voices.

Equipment

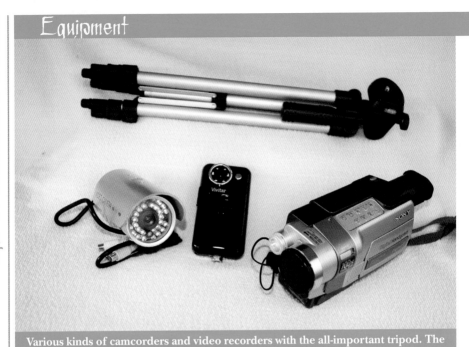

Various kinds of camcorders and video recorders with the all-important tripod. The small one also has night vision and is used during vigils for isolating small areas while moving from room to room.

CAMCORDER
Either tape or digital.

These are great to set up in a room and let run.

- Always have spare tapes and batteries.

- Home base is where monitors and recorders of all kinds are located. This helps insure that your equipment is working during the course of the paranormal investigation. This is more of a luxury than necessity at first. You will review the tapes or DVDs anyway later. These take the longest to set up and put into action. We use small handheld camcorders in the spots where the cameras will be placed for recording onto DVD. This way we lose no chance of capturing a paranormal occurrence. We have seen inexperienced investigators take up to 45 minutes to set up their camera. Do you realize how much activity could transpire in that time? Most of the activity we have experienced has happened in a matter of seconds. Again, the ghosts or spirits are not going to sit there waiting for you to get ready for them.

- Don't forget a tripod if you have one.

This snake camera can help locate rational explanations to possible haunts by reaching into places that are difficult to see. The camera at the end of the flexible snake has an adjustable light and the monitor is removable with a multi-angle feature.

CAMERA

A staple of the modern ghost hunter. *(See below for more information.)*

- Ask the spirits for permission to photograph them while loading film at the same time. For some reason, there has been a high success rate due to this act. Perhaps the spirits enjoy politeness, who knows?

- If you have a digital camera, ask while setting it up.

- Take lots of pictures. We use film because the negatives are HARD PROOF. There is a cost issue that goes with it. Digital gives you results of your photos in seconds but the digital zoom on these cameras seem to capture a lot of "orbs." That is due to the zoom moving in on the first thing that moves and usually it is a dust orb, water droplet, even a snowflake. That is why so many people have suddenly captured so many orbs on camera when before with the manual focus 35 mm cameras they were rare. It is good to have both if you can but not completely necessary. We also use digital SLR (single lens reflex) cameras. These are the best of both worlds, manual focus of a 35 mm and digital pictures. They are, however, a bit expensive.

- Always say "FLASH" before taking photos with other people in the room. That way they can look away and not see spots for the next few minutes.

Equipment

Small Inexpensive But Worthwhile Items

Wind chimes are also called "Ghost Catchers." They will signal any movement from energy or drafts. These can be purchased anywhere. Motion detectors are another way of catching movement but are a bit more expensive.

Balloons can also help locate unseen drafts.

Tape and thread can be put on windows, drawers, doors, or across doorways to find out if your haunt is real or someone's folly.

Baby powder can be spread on floors. Ghosts can leave marks or prints but so can people and critters.

Tape measures can help measure distances when necessary.

Watch: You can time durations of phenomena or a person's watch of an area.

Compasses come in handy when spirits drain EMF detectors or the EMF fields are too active due to faulty wiring or lots of electrical equipment in an area. When something is trying to manifest, the compass needle will swing in the direction of activity.

Regular thermometers are foolproof. They do not run on batteries that can be drained during paranormal activity. Also take air temperature.

Area maps or a **drawn outline** of site in question.

Labels and **bags or vials** for evidence and marking the specimens. They can also be used to label area in question. We use contact lens vials from weekly cleaner kits.

Chalk is used to outline items that are reported to move in a haunting. That way we can track and measure any movement during the paranormal investigation. Powder is very smooth and can cause the item to slide on its own. Never put an item on top of powder to track its movement or you will get false results. Any small vibration will cause movement.

Small levels are very handy for helping determine why things might move. Tables or other items that are not level will obviously cause items that are on them to move.

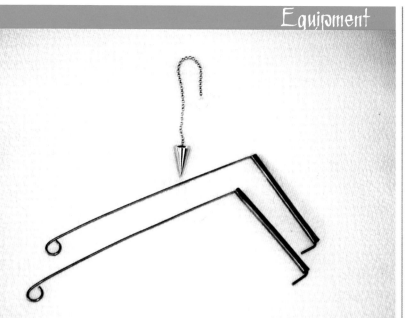

Dowsing rods and pendulums have become very popular in spirit communication. No one is sure how the tools work, not even the experts who use them, but they do work and have proven effective as a safe, positive form of communicating or finding places where energy is present.

DOWSING RODS & PENDULUMS
Easy to use and among the oldest of detectors.

- You do not have to be psychic or magical to master them.

- Becoming increasingly available. We bought our first set and then made the others. No one, even dowsers are sure how they work but they do. Water companies carry dowsing rods in their trucks to find water mains. We use them to see if there is any energy present and also try to get some answers that might help us pinpoint the historical timeline of a haunt. This enables us to communicate with a better knowledge of the time the spirits or ghosts may have lived. The spirit of a person that lived in 1750 may not have any knowledge of a recorder or DVD player but may be very familiar with hoops or ninepin. We have used this method with amazing results and will continue to do so.

Before an Investigation

Find out the history of the place in question. Get names and dates of interest. Interview the people involved or who might have knowledge of the site.

- What have they seen? How Often?

- What time does the occurrences take place?

- What were the conditions both inside and outside?

- What were their personal conditions at the time(s) of the occurrence(s)?

- What did the apparition if there was one, look like?

- Did it acknowledge your presence?

- Did it speak to you or move?

Make sure they are very thorough in their descriptions. Be very thorough in your notes of their answers. You are looking for a spirit profile. This determines consistent patterns that the haunting might take on. You can use this to do your investigation at the most opportune time with maximum results.

Another important aspect when interviewing people is not to lead them on. In other words, if they say they saw an apparition, let them describe it. Do not ask if it was white, hazy, or wearing certain clothes. This act tends to create a preconceived notion where you are actually placing a different picture in their head that may be nothing like what they actually witnessed. We always let the witnesses

of the paranormal activity talk away and record their every word. If you fill in any blanks, then you are basically creating something that is not really there.

We were at an investigation one time where Arlene asked the woman what did the apparition look like? She answered that it looked rather old fashioned. Another investigator piped in and said, "So the ghost you saw was dressed in colonial period clothing with a dark colored suit on. The woman, now had that vision in her head as she answered, "Yes, kind of." Had he left her to completely describe her ghost, she may have had a bit different and more accurate description of the apparition. It may have not been colonial at all, but it was now.

Other very important questions to ask are:

- How old is the place in question?

- Is there an attic? A basement?

- Are there water pipes that make noise? What kind of heating system?

- Is there a pond or stream nearby?

- What happens before and after the occurrences?

- Where are the occurrences most common?

These should get you going as to whether there is a legitimate reason to investigate or not.

Arrive early and pick a room or spot of least activity for home base. This is where you will keep your equipment, bags, monitors, etc. Get set up and make a sweep of the place. If it is a cemetery, check out everything within a fifty-yard radius.

Begin with your meters, recorder, and camera. If you get something out of the ordinary, take pictures and record immediately. Just remember, glossy areas such as windows, mirrors, painted walls, tombstones, and other shiny surfaces will create strange patterns, as will reflections from flashlights and outside sources. Make sure you keep notes of any such things for later.

Always make notes of strange noises or lights that are not paranormal. I make notes right on the recorder as I am doing EVP recordings. That way I know later it was natural and not paranormal. Remember, we are always looking for rational explanations to occurrences. It is when the rational runs out that we begin to work towards the paranormal.

Do not go into a place a skeptic. This already puts you in a negative position. At the same time do not enter a place believing it is haunted. This might cause you to jump to conclusions. Be an open-minded detective and work out any evidence from a neutral and knowledgeable standpoint.

If you enter a room with a video camera in it, let home base know. This way, your out of camera view noises will not be mistaken for paranormal phenomena.

You do not need the lights out. That is a great television special effect and nothing else. However, if the activity occurs only when a room or area is dark, you do want to recreate that scenario for best results. Again, this is where doing your homework and proper interviewing in regard to the haunting pays off.

Do not be afraid to experiment during a ghost hunt or investigation. Ask the ghosts to appear, or sing an old song. Try conversation. In the end, you never know from investigation to investigation what is going to work in each particular case. We try to use every bit of equipment and tactic mentioned to lure the ghosts out. Ghost hunting is like fishing. You must be patient and have intuition to be successful. Yes, in the end, your intuition and homework will pay off. *You* are the most valuable ghost-hunting tool you have.

Always be polite and touch nothing. Always be silent and move as little as possible if someone is attempting EVPs. Professionalism gets more results.

Many paranormal investigators log the activity of the sun and moon. Solar flares can disrupt the geomagnetic field in and around the earth. These disruptions have been affiliated with elevated paranormal activity. Many paranormal websites give the celestial activity in small boxes. Flares are labeled as solar x-rays and if present, the box will say "active." If not, it will say "normal." If they are disrupting the earth's geomagnetic field, the box will say "storm." If not, it will say "quiet." The moon's phases are also a factor in spirit activity. The full and new moons seem to conjure up the most activity. Make note of these for comparing later investigations and any activity intensity.

RULES OF INVESTIGATION

- Never whisper. People taking EVPs might mistake your voice for paranormal. You will not scare the ghosts by talking in a normal voice. Do not talk loud though, just enough to be heard and logged as not paranormal in nature.

- When others are recording EVPs, be as quiet as possible. Even shuffling around or moving items can sound like an EVP later.

- Record in short frames. We usually record for about 5 minutes before moving to the next room or area. Lets face it, how many random questions would you want to answer before you got bored and left? Ask a question and wait 10-15 seconds before asking the next question. We also engage in plain conversation as if the spirit was with us at a gathering. This way the energy may feel more comfortable to mingle and communicate.

- Never ask questions such as "How did you die?" In some cases the spirits don't know they are dead and you will not get an answer.

- Do not scold, yell, or demand ghosts to show a sign. We have seen amateur investigators bang on walls and demand the ghosts to show themselves or they will be punished. This IS amateur and very unprofessional. Would you listen to them?

- Ask positive and friendly questions. Our friend and expert investigator Matt Moniz of spookysouthcoast.com suggests that you give a polite greeting, and ask questions such as:

Hello, how are you?

My name is _____.
What's your name?

What is new with you?

Do you have any children?

Do you have a spouse?

What is your favorite food?

What is your favorite color?

Perhaps invite them to finish or join in on an old saying or song.

- Try to find out any relevant facts that might help pinpoint the era of the spirit or ghost you are trying to communicate with. It is useless to talk about automobiles to a spirit from the eighteenth century or tell them to make your EMF meter go off. They did not have electricity or EMF meters back then so how would they know what to do with them?

- Don't be afraid to get creative. If you know something about the particular spirit, such as the spirit was reported in the booth at the tavern, ask questions such as "Who are you waiting for?" or "Is there something you would like to tell us?" Assure them that you mean no harm and would like to help them.

- Digital or film cameras are acceptable. Professional equipment is not necessary. We have seen disposable cameras get the same results as professional equipment.

- Always say, "FLASH" or "PIC" before shooting a picture so others can look away and preserve their night adjusted eye focus. No one wants to walk around for a few minutes during an investigation with bright spots in their eyes.

- Try not to get into each other's photos unless they want you there. Sometimes activity gravitates around a person and shows up on film. Don't worry if the person is not in full frame or focus. They are not the subject of the photo, they are just part of the photo background.

- Always take immediate pictures where there are temperature drops or meter fluctuations but beware of condensation forming from water vapor (fog/mist) that can be mistaken for ectoplasm, orbs, or other paranormal phenomena.

- Ghosts may appear as mist, ectoplasm, apparitions, or orbs. But remember, what appears to be "orbs" can actually be dust, moisture, insects, shutter malfunction, or underexposure. Dust, water vapor, and other false orbs have a semi-hollow look or appear to be halo-like light. True orbs are lit from within and cast shadows, and can be colored. During an investigation at the Houghton Mansion in North Adams, four of us watched orbs floating about us that were green, yellow, red, and white. Though orbs are not a true indicator that a place is haunted, a haunted place does have orbs reported within the area.

- Night vision/night shot cameras have the ability to take photos in very low light and can be very useful. Most of these cameras have a CCD or charged coupled device that amplifies the available light. These should not be confused with thermal imaging that relies on detecting heat.

- Video recordings may require two times the review work. The first is done with the sound off in order to focus on the visual alone. Look for all the known false evidence such as dust, fog, insects, etc. and keep a sharp watch for faint reflections off shiny objects as well. Look for the slightest change in the frames. The second should be done with the sound up to detect any EVPs that may have been recorded.

Common Mistakes to Avoid

1. **Do not trespass.** Be respectful of private property. Ask permission. Do not litter. Leave an area the way it looked when you arrived.

2. **Never go alone.** This applies in case of injury. Also, if you witness something, you have a partner to back up your sighting. Always let someone know where you will be and carry an ID. Even if you have permission to be somewhere, the proper authorities might still question you.

3. **Test all your equipment before you go to a site.** Make sure you know how to use the equipment before even thinking of trying it on the job. Put fresh batteries in everything.

4. **Check out sites in the day so you can get a basic idea of what to expect if you go back at night.** Carry a notebook and log every little detail no matter how seemingly small.

5. **You do not have to whisper during an investigation.** Do not whisper when doing EVP recordings. You might confuse your voice with that of something else. You will not scare the ghosts by using a normal clear voice. Hopefully, they will not scare you either.

6. **Research, research, research.** If you do not know what you are looking for, how do you expect to find it?

7. **Bring only what you need for that particular case.** Obviously, a base camp is useless a mile into the woods where a haunted ruin might be and there is no electricity. Again, research will provide you with the necessary equipment so you are not bogged down with too much useless stuff.

8. **Bring food and drinks with you.** Everybody gets hungry and thirsty. You need your energy to find the other energy.

9. **Do not go into places that are dangerous.** Some places are disasters waiting for a victim. As an investigator, you must be prudent and realize that a collapsing building or slippery ledge is just not worth becoming a ghost over.

10. **Do not wear cologne or perfumes.** Many times that is a sign of a haunting and you might interfere. Also, if you are in the woods, it might attract insects. If you use bug spray, make sure it is odorless and log its use. Always wear clothing conducive to the area you will be in. Do not wear bright clothes in a building as you might reflect light causing a false reading. On the other hand, if in the woods wear something appropriate for proper identification in case hunters are out. Simple good judgment will always obtain better results.

The following page is a sample ghost-hunting log we have devised for our investigations. These are very important as they give us an idea from investigation to investigation as to what may be common occurrences in certain situations. We can compare the records and this helps us in determining what has statistically happened during moon phases, certain changes in the geometric field, weather patterns, things we tried in order to get some sort of communication from the energy in certain places, and other factors. Feel free to copy it of create your own based on this model for your specific needs.

Date _____ Time _____
Location _____
Number of rooms _____
Investigators_____
Weather _____
Moon Phase _____Solar Activity _____

EQUIPMENT

Cameras & Film_____
Audio Recorders _____
Video Cameras _____
EMF Meters

EMF METER	READING	ROOM

Thermometers

THERMOMETER	READING	ROOM

DVD / VCR Recorders

DVD	VCR	RECORDER	LENGTH
☐	☐		
☐	☐		

Other Equipment

PHENOMENA DURING INVESTIGATION

TIME	PHENOMENA

Conclusion

There are many perennial favorites that have been omitted from this writing for several reasons. One is that the haunt may either no longer exist, or the owners wish not to be bothered by those seeking signs of the afterlife. Another is that the places since other writings, have been either debunked or never existed in the first place. Some may exist but their tales of ghosts and things that go bump in the night were merely tall yarns fabricated way back when a ghost story had much more impetus while being narrated in front of the crackling fires that once warmed New England homes. Others have been told so many times, they are a main staple in the realm of haunted New England. In this case, other authors have told them sufficiently and there is no reason to reiterate them here.

Perhaps you will find some new places that will someday soon become the talk on dark cold nights in New England when the moon is full and the crackling fire muffles the sounds of what lurks just beyond your eyes and ears.

Resources

www.dorsetinn.com

www.ghostvillage.com

www.flickr.com

www.foodforthedead.com

www.joenickell.com

www.neara.org

www.norwichinn.com

www.shadowlands.com

www.shardvilla.org

www.svc.edu/history/index.html

www.Vermonter.com

www.oldstagecoach.com

www.celebrateboston.com

www.Equinoxresort.com

www.greenmountaininn.com

www.dorsetinn.com

www.norwichinn.com

www.vermonthistory.org

www.zerotime.com

Bibliography

Balzano, Christopher. Picture Yourself Ghost Hunting. Boston, MA: Course Technology, 2009.

Belanger, Jeff. Encyclopedia of Haunted Places. Franklin Lakes, NJ: New Page Books, 2005.

Bell, Michael E. Food for the Dead. New York, NY: Carroll & Graf Publishers, 2001.

Botkin, B.A. A Treasury of New England Folklore. New York: Bonanza Books, 1995.

Bolte', Mary and Eastman, Mary. Haunted New England. Riverside, CT: Chatham Press Inc., 1972.

Cahill, Robert Ellis. New England's Ancient Mysteries. Salem, MA: Old Saltbox Publishing House, 1993.

Cahill, Robert Ellis. New England's Mountain Madness. Peabody, MA: Chandler-Smith Publishing, 1989.

Citro, Joseph. Green Mountain Dark Tales. Hanover, NH: University Press of New England, 1999.

Citro, Joseph. Green Mountain Ghosts, Ghouls, & Unsolved Mysteries. New York, NY: Houghton Mifflin Company, 1994.

Citro, Joseph. Passing Strange. Boston, MA: Houghton Mifflin Company, 1996.

D'Agostino, Thomas. A Guide to Haunted New England: Tales from Mount Washington to the Newport Cliffs. Charleston, SC: History Press, 2009.

D'Agostino, Thomas. A History of Vampires in New England. Charleston, SC: History Press, 2010.

D'Agostino, Thomas. Abandoned Villages and Ghost Towns of New England. Atglen, PA: Schiffer Publishing LTD, 2008.

Dix, Bryon E. and Mavor, James W. Manitou: The Sacred Landscape of New England's Native Civilization. Rochester, VT: Inner Traditions, 1989.

Drake, Samuel Adams. New England Legends and Folklore. Boston, MA: Little, Brown, and Company, 1883.

BIBLIOGRAPHY

Fell, Barry. America B.C.: Ancient Settlers in the New World. New York, NY: Simon and Schuster, 1989.

Fusco, C.J. Old Ghosts of New England. Woodstock, VT: The Countryman Press, 2009.

Hauck, Dennis William. Haunted Places; The National Directory. New York, NY: Penguin Books, 1996.

Jasper, Mark. Haunted Inns of New England. Yarmouthport, MA: On Cape Publications, 2000.

Lewis, Thea. Haunted Burlington – Spirits of Vermont's Queen City. Charleston, SC: History Press, 2009.

Mansfield, David L. The History of the Town of Dummerston. Vermont Historical Magazine, 1884.

McCain, Diana Ross. Mysteries and Legends of New England. Guilford, CT: Globe Pequot Press, 2009.

Pitkin, David. Ghosts of the Northeast. Salem, NY: Aurora Publications, 2002.

Rondina, Christopher. The Vampire Hunter's Guide to New England. North Attleborough, MA: Covered Bridge Press, 2000.

Schlosser, S.E. Spooky New England. Guilford, CT. Globe Pequot Press, 2004.

Smith, Terry L. and Jean, Mark. Haunted Inns of America. Crane Hill Publishers, 2003.

Smitten, Susan. Ghost Stories of New England. Auburn, WA: Ghost House Books, 2003.

Wood, Maureen and Kolek, Ron. The Ghost Chronicles. Naperville, Il Sourcebooks Inc., 2009.